Praise for Healthy Relationships…

"This book is full of interesting and relevant information on building healthy relationships. The format is easy to use and helps readers make valuable connections to their personal lives. *Healthy Relationships* can have a tremendous impact on the lives of impressionable young adults."
Amy Summers-Special Education Teacher

"*Healthy Relationships* is a guide that can be used to help anyone who wants to improve their interactions. The strategies are easily applied and support positive relationships."
Sally Condie-Special Education IA

"*Healthy Relationships* is very well thought-out. In fact, I found myself not just reading but really paying attention to the tips in the book and storing them in my brain to use when I confront a friendship/dating situation in my life. I also found myself answering the questions in the book as they apply to me. I thought the acronym (SNAIL) and the different steps were useful and will help people who encounter these situations in life."
Elizabeth Alper-Student

"This is a very useful book, I am using it with the young adult minded women, ages 24 to 43, in the group home in which I work. The workbook format makes it easy to guide them through concrete steps to support forming lasting friendships and relationships. They often refer back to the book when they have questions and enjoy repeating activities. The chapter on safety has changed everyone's perspective on how to navigate relationships. The women are much more mindful of protecting their safety and now have exit plans established. Thank you!"
Beverley Alanjary- Group Home Advisor

"The information in this book is useful and easily applicable to every day experiences. It is hard to maintain friendships. By completing the activities and following the SNAIL tips, building life-long friendships becomes more doable."
Cierra Bantz- Student

"*Healthy Relationships* provides many helping tools that are perfect for supporting special needs students. Navigating social relationships is difficult for many, and it is nice to have a guide to support students in developing necessary social skills."
Angela Mataafa- Special Education IA

"*Healthy Relationships* is a book like <u>7 Habits of Highly Effective People</u>. It's relevant every day of our lives. As our relationships grow naturally, the tips and strategies in the book ensure that our relationships grow in a positive and healthy manner. It's a good idea to repeat and review this book often. The Snail Talk and Snail Wisdom are spot on!"
Julia M. Uhll-Parent and Advocate

Healthy Relationships

A guide book for teens and adults with Williams Syndrome, Autism, ADHD, Intellectual Disabilities, Learning Disabilities and other human conditions that may present challenges in building Healthy Relationships!

We dedicate this workbook to all who realize that **being** the right person is as important as **finding** the right person.

Be the person you want to find!

This product is not a substitute for psychological, professional, or parental advice. If psychological or other expert assistance is required, the services of a competent professional person should be sought. The authors and publisher are not responsible for errors or omissions or for any application of the information of this book and make no warranty, either implied or expressed, with regard to the content of this book.

Copyright © 2013 Diana Loiewski, M.Ed. and Tarane Sondoozi, Psy.D.

All rights reserved. The material contained herein is protected by copyright. No part of it may be republished, copied, reproduced, or transmitted in any form by electronic or mechanical means, including information storage and retrieval systems, without permission in writing from the publisher.

Printed in the United States of America

Published by Talkcounts LLC
P.O. Box 503293
San Diego, CA. 92150

www.talkcounts.com

ISBN: 978-0-9852491-2-0

Cover Design and Art Direction: Linda Loiewski

Comics and Layout Support: Miriam Larson

Executive Editor: Kari Palm

Editor: Kathryn Galloway

Introduction

Building friendships and creating a **Healthy Relationship** takes time, takes patience, and takes commitment. What people want from relationships can vary from a simple friendship to looking for long-term commitments. Getting to know someone and developing shared interests is often difficult. It requires not only self-awareness and knowing what you want, but also knowing what the other person in the relationship wants. To suceed, you must be curious and view relationships as an investigative process. Building a **Healthy Relationship** is a learning process that involves two people who are curious about themselves and each other. Through spending time with each other in a variety of settings, they create experiences that can help them decide if they want to continue the relationship and work toward mutual goals.

For the most part, as long as the people involved in the relationship are honest, willing to communicate openly and they agree on what they are willing to give and take from each other, the relationship works. **Healthy Relationships** don't just happen. They take time, effort, work, and continuous communication. To really get to know someone requires interacting with the other person in a variety of different settings. **Healthy Relationships** require investigating and knowing as much as you can about the other person's history. Getting to know someone's history can help you predict their future behavior. This workbook is designed to help you understand how to build and maintain a **Healthy Relationship**.

Many chapters contain special words and their definitions can be found at the end of the supplied CD-ROM. These words and their definitions are important to learn so that you can clearly understand the ideas that are presented. We encourage you to cut the words out and use them as you read and complete the activities. Once defined, each word will have the same meaning throughout the workbook. Additionally, IEP goals can be found in a chapter on the CD-ROM.

You will see the bolded word **Activity** throughout the workbook. It is recommended that when you see it, you stop and complete the activity. The activities are meant to guide you and prepare your thinking about a concept or idea on which you are working. In addition, there are opportunities for marking multiple check boxes. Please place check marks in all of the boxes that apply to you.

Comics are provided within chapters. Comic strips illustrate and teach concepts and also provide opportunities for discussion.

This workbook is really a thinking tool to help you build **Healthy Relationships**. We want you to make it your own—write all over it, cross things out and underline it in three different colors: add as you will.

Although we think that our readers are primarily young adults, your parents, older siblings, and friends who are single or trying to improve their relationships can also benefit from this book. Feel free to show them this workbook. Better yet, encourage them to get one of their own. After all, this particular workbook is uniquely yours.

Table of Contents

1. The SNAIL is Our Mascot……………………………………………..1

- Reasons for Choosing the SNAIL

2. Safety First……………………………………………………............9

- Tell, Take & Look (TTL)
- Pink Flags & Red Flags

3. Knowing What You Want…………………………………………..29

- Attributes & Characteristics

4. Wash it, Brush it, and Tuck it……………………………………...39

- Levels of Personal Hygiene

5. Meeting Someone New……………………………………………..47

- Enjoying One Another's Company

6. Relationships Take Time and Effort……………………………….69

- Shared Trust
- Shared Respect
- Effective Communication
- Shared Goals
- Becoming Friends

7. Sweet Emotions…………………………………………………….103

- Crush vs Love

8. **Deal Breakers**..113
   - The Five Deal Breakers

9. **It's More than T.R.U.S.T**...123
   - Gathering Information for Your Safety

10. **Physical Intimacy**..131
    - Finding and Being the Right Person

11. **Parent/Guardian Advice**...139

12. **Wrapping it Up**..143

Chapter 1

The SNAIL is Our Mascot

Reason for Choosing the SNAIL

The SNAIL is Our Mascot

Having a symbol that represents a concept is a great way to remember the lessons that this workbook is teaching. Our mascot is a **SNAIL** and you will learn our reasons for adopting the **SNAIL** and the strategies necessary for keeping yourself safe.

We have created an acronym for you to remember the importance of the **SNAIL**.

Slow down

Make sure you understand yourself and the other person that you are with. Set expectations.

Negotiate

Work out and agree on rules for your relationships (we call this the **Code of Conduct**).

Ask

Question how your choices and behaviors will affect the other person, and your relationship. Always attend to the **Pink** and **Red Flags**.

Investigate

Look closely at the other person before you decide to pursue a relationship.

Listen

Listen to your heart and to what your partner is saying with their words and actions.

Reasons for Choosing the SNAIL

- The snail moves slowly and takes time to lay its path so that it can travel safely. **Healthy Relationships** need to move slowly as the couple learns about one another and creates a safe environment for each other.

- The snail paves its own way and protects its belly (where it is most vulnerable) by creating and leaving a trail. This path protects the snail's body and shows where it has been. So remember, you create your own path and you impact the lives of people with whom you interact. You're responsible for your own safety and for the safety of the hearts with whom you connect. To choose the safest path takes time and thought.

- The snail's shell looks a lot like the inner part of the human ear. An important part of any **Healthy Relationship** is listening. You must listen to yourself, to your heart and to your friend to hear what he/she is saying and feeling.

- The snail's shell is a never-ending spiral, a series of circles within each other representing the different steps in your relationships. All the steps in building **Healthy Relationships** are related.

- The snail carries its personal space or home on its back. Other snails can't occupy it. This is how it creates and sets clear boundaries. The same applies when building **Healthy Relationships**. As close as we may feel to someone, setting appropriate boundaries will ensure that both parties' needs are met equally. **Healthy Relationships** ultimately help you become a better person and enriches your inner world as well as your life.

Activity

Identify our SNAIL

First, complete each letter from our acronym! If you need help, see the preceding page. Second, complete the following questions under each letter. Later, with your friend/date share the questions and together discuss the answers:

S_____

How can I build a friendship? (Check the boxes in the following activities.)

☐ Exchange phone numbers and arrange for a time to speak on the phone.

☐ Invite the person to spend more time with me.

☐ Hang out with this person at my home.

What are the things that I like to do?

_____

_____

What is important to me in a friendship?

☐ We will keep each other's secrets.

☐ We will keep each other safe.

☐ We will be honest.

☐ We will develop common goals.

N_____

_____

What do you think the rules of the friendship should be?

☐ Do what you say you're going to do.

☐ Be respectful.

☐ Be trustworthy.

☐ Be honest.

☐ Be drug free.

I can figure out the rules of a friendship with another person by:

☐ Having a discussion about what is important in our friendship.

☐ Spending time with the other person in different settings and talking about how we like to be treated.

What should I do if I told someone how I want to be treated and they don't treat me that way?

☐ Work with the person to fix the situation.

☐ Look at my actions in the situation.

☐ Ask the other person for his/her side of the story.

☐ Respectfully let the other person know how I feel.

A_____

_____

What do I need to know about the other person to make sure that I am safe in the friendship?

_____

_____

What should I tell my friends about myself to make sure that I am safe in the friendship?

- [ ] How I would like to be treated.
- [ ] What I like and don't like.
- [ ] How I like to be contacted.
- [ ] My interests and hobbies.

I_____

_____

To protect my safety, I need to pay attention to:

- [ ] My friend's behavior towards me.
- [ ] How my friend treats others.

L_____

_____

I need to listen to my friend and make sure that what he/she says and does are the same. How can I do that?

_____

_____

_____

One of the most important ways that we can earn someone's trust is by making sure that what he/she says and does are the same. To decide if a person's words and actions match, think about these steps:
1- What are they saying and committing to do?
2- Do they follow through?
3- Do their actions match what they say?
4- Do they have a legitimate reason for not following through?
5- Do their reasons make sense?

What are they saying and committing to do?	Do they follow through?	Does their action match what they say?	What are the possible reasons for not following through?
A person tells you they will call you later. The person calls.	Yes ☐ No ☐	Yes ☐ No ☐	
A person tells you that they will bring you something that you need. He/she doesn't bring what you needed.	Yes ☐ No ☐	Yes ☐ No ☐	
A person agrees to meet you at the mall at three o'clock and they are there.	Yes ☐ No ☐	Yes ☐ No ☐	
A person agrees to help you complete a project and they don't.	Yes ☐ No ☐	Yes ☐ No ☐	
A person tells you that you can get together on the weekend and you do.	Yes ☐ No ☐	Yes ☐ No ☐	

Give an example of when your words and actions didn't match: For instance, when you promised that you would do something that you didn't do.

_____

_____

Did you have a good reason for not following through?   Yes ☐   No ☐

Did you tell the other person your reason? Yes ☐   No ☐

Did your reason for not following through make sense to the other person?

_____

_____

Give an example when someone's word and actions didn't match: For instance when he/she didn't do what he/she promised.

_____

_____

Did he/she have a good reason for not following through?   Yes ☐   No ☐

Did he/she tell you the reason? Yes ☐   No ☐

Did his/her reason for not following through make sense to you?

_____

_____

When someone doesn't do what they say, how does it affect your relationship?

☐ It hurts my feelings.

☐ It breaks my trust.

☐ I feel disrespected.

So remember our mascot the **SNAIL** and what each letter represents. They are simple but effective ways to keep yourself, the other person, and the relationship healthy and safe.

- **S**low down: make sure you understand yourself and the other person that you are with. Set expectations.

- **N**egotiate: list all of the ways that you want to behave (we call this the **Code of Conduct**) in your relationship.

- **A**sk: question how your choices and behaviors affect the other person and your relationship. Always attend to the **Pink** and **Red Flags**.

- **I**nvestigate: look closely at the other person before you decide to pursue a relationship.

- **L**isten: listen to your heart and to what your partner is saying with their words and actions.

Throughout this workbook, you will see **Snail Talk** and **Snail Wisdom**. These are opportunities for you to think about and reflect on the author's advice. **Snail Trails** are stories that will help you understand and learn about building **Healthy Relationships**. All of the stories are made up. The names and scenarios are all fictitious.

Chapter 2

Safety First

Tell, Take, & Look (TTL)

Pink Flags & Red Flags

Safety First

Your safety needs to be your priority. When you were younger it was your parents' job to keep you safe, and now it is your responsibility. There are several things that you need to do at **all times** to make sure that you are safe while building friendships and dating relationships. In this chapter you will learn the importance of recognizing **Pink** and **Red Flags** and you will be provided with many scenarios to practice reacting to situations that may occur while building **Healthy Relationships**.

Tell, Take, & Look. (TTL)

Our number one rule is safety first. You must be safe at all times and in order to do this you must: **Tell, Take,** & **Look. (TTL)**
- Always **Tell** someone where you are going and with whom.
- Always **Take** some form of communication device so that you can inform someone if your plans change.
- Always **Look** around; know where you are, and have an exit plan.

Realize that when you first meet someone he/she becomes an acquaintance. **An acquaintance is someone that you don't really know.** You may recognize an acquaintance and know his/her name but you most likely have never been to his/her home. **An acquaintance is a stranger.** You don't know much about each other. You don't know his/her likes, background, or history. Even if you have known or been in contact through Social Media or texting for a long period of time, he/she is still a stranger. Relationships with acquaintances can lead to friendships.

Snail Wisdom

Remember, a person that you meet over Social Media is still an acquaintance until you meet him/her in person, meet their family and friends, and get to know them. You must be careful and remember that relationships are built slowly and over time.

Say this to yourself three times: **RELATIONSHIPS ARE BUILT SLOWLY AND OVER TIME.**

We are also responsible for how we behave towards others. There are certain behaviors that can create an uneasy feeling in others and make them feel unsafe around you. Staring or following people who you don't really know are two ways that cause others to feel uncomfortable.

> Snail Trail...
>
> John is very attracted to girls with blonde hair. Sometimes when he sees a girl with blonde hair, he will stand by her side and stare, especially if he thinks he knows her. He will look at her for a long time without moving his eyes or talking with her.

 Snail Talk

Staring is very bad behavior. When people are stared at, they feel uncomfortable and want to leave the situation. John should never stare at someone just because he likes her. A relationship involves two people liking each other. Staring at someone that you don't know is creepy.

Activity
Staring

Staring at someone you don't know is considered inappropriate behavior and it will not help you to make a friend. When you catch yourself staring, consider looking away or introducing yourself. You can then compliment the person on the quality that they have that is making you stare.

How can staring get you into trouble?

_____

_____

_____

Staring is considered to be a rude behavior. Sometimes people stare when they hear a noise, or when they see something or someone that looks strange. However, that doesn't mean that staring is okay to do.

Instead you may want to apologize for staring and then share why with a compliment. Example: "Please forgive me for staring. I just really like your outfit."

Activity

Conversation starters: place a check next to the statements that you might be comfortable saying to someone that you would like to meet.

- [ ] Cool watch.
- [ ] Nice shoes.
- [ ] Where did you get your hair cut?
- [ ] You look familiar.
- [ ] Do we know one another?
- [ ] Can you believe the weather that we are having?
- [ ] Where did you buy your outfit?

Additionally, if you catch yourself staring you may want to look away towards something else or talk to a person that you are with.

List some things you can do instead of staring:

_____

_____

If you think you see someone that you recognize from class, club, church/temple (religious place of worship) or the community, instead of staring, you can approach him/her and ask if you know one another.

If the person says, "No," what should you do?

_____

_____

_____

If you see someone that you would like to meet, what could you say?

_____

_____

_____

List the things you can say or do if you catch someone staring at you:

_____

_____

_____

Say this to yourself three times: **STARING IS NOT OKAY. I HAVE OTHER OPTIONS.**

SNAIL Trail…

Julie has a job at the grocery store and during break she followed a boy into the break room to look at him. She stared at him, and the boy left the room immediately.

SNAIL Talk

Julie needs to be careful about following people just because she is attracted to them. Most people do not like to be followed, and it sends a bad message. This type of behavior is known as stalking and it is illegal in most states. Instead, Julie should try to have a conversation and make friends with the boy.

What should you do if you believe someone is following you?

_____

_____

_____

How can you tell that someone is interested in being your friend?

☐ You exchange phone numbers.

☐ You invite one another to meet again.

☐ You talk with the person.

☐ You share the same interests.

How can you tell that someone is **NOT** interested in being your friend?

☐ He/she doesn't speak with you.

☐ He/she doesn't share the same interests.

☐ He/she doesn't make arrangements to meet again.

☐ He/she hangs out with different people than you do.

Making a friend is much like dancing a slow dance. Each person has to be careful not to move too fast and each person needs to be aware of what the other person is doing and feeling. You wouldn't want to step on each other's toes. Instead, you want to step carefully and make sure that you are respectful and are working together to dance well.

Activity
The difference between an acquaintance and a friend

List the names of your friends:

_____

_____

_____

List the people in your life that are acquaintance:

_____

_____

_____

What is the difference between your friends and your acquaintances?

_____

_____

_____

How did your acquaintances become friends?

_____

_____

_____

What types of activities do you like to do with your friends?

_____

_____

_____

SNAIL Wisdom

Pay attention to Pink Flags. Pink Flags are those little things that we may recognize or know as our inner voice. Pink Flags warn us that something is wrong or may go wrong with someone else or in a situation. Pink Flags are our signal to investigate what we are sensing further. As you investigate, if you notice what you are sensing becomes stronger, you need to realize that the Pink Flag is really a Red Flag. Red Flags indicate that you must distance yourself. In fact, all Red Flags and some Pink Flags tell you to distance yourself. To distance yourself means to limit contact with the person until you can further investigate them.

Let's review...

Acquaintances can lead to friendships. As you get to know one another over time, you investigate each other to see what things you have in common. You share interests and spend time together. One of the best ways to build relationships is by remembering what the other person shares with you and what you experience together. Remembering what took place the last time you met creates a bond and makes people feel thought about. You may find yourself developing common goals and common interests. You have fun together and enjoy one another's company.

When you are honest, you develop trust in one another. If you sense a **Pink Flag** you need to pause and discuss your concerns and ask questions. You continue to investigate the relationship, and if too many **Pink Flags** come up along the way, or if you decide that your values are too different, the friendship may end.

Friendships are very important and it takes work to build friendships. Some friendships move into dating relationships, and the investigation of one another continues to happen over time.

Think of one of your acquaintances and list two things you can talk with him/her about:

_____

_____

Think of one of your acquaintances and list two things that he/she have shared with you in the past:

_____

_____

Acquaintance and Friend Chart.

Put a check in the boxes that acquaintance and friends have in common. The first one is done for you.

Things in common	Acquaintance	Friends
Connected on Social Media	✓	✓
Face is familiar		
See them around		
May have friends in common		
Know each other's phone number		
Know each other's address		
Know his/her family		
Know/share favorite activities		
Know his/her likes and dislikes		
Trusting and feeling safe with each other		
Taking care of each other's needs		
Concerned about each other's safety		

What are some of the things that you can do to move your relationship from an acquaintance to a friendship?

- ☐ Invite the acquaintance to my home to meet my family.
- ☐ Communicate more with him/her on the phone.
- ☐ Make plans with him/her.
- ☐ Do activities outside of our homes.
- ☐ Develop common interests.

As we said previously (**SNAIL Wisdom** on page 16) **Pink Flags** are those feelings that warn us that something is wrong or may go wrong. Most times we choose to ignore, forgive, or forget **Pink Flags**. Instead, we need to realize that **Pink Flags** are small but important signals that we experience with each other. If we ignore them, they may eventually lead to **Red Flags** and can create disappointment, drama, and pain.

For example, Jeff was about to dive into the pool and had a funny feeling that the pool may not be deep enough and yet he jumped. Unfortunately, he did not listen to the funny feeling; consequently, he hit his head on the bottom. Had he listened to his inner voice and checked out how deep the pool actually was, he would have avoided the pain and injury.

Describe some of the **Pink Flags** that you have either experienced or seen on television:

_____

_____

Think about a scary movie. What happens when the **Pink Flags** are ignored?

- ☐ Characters react in a frightened manner.
- ☐ Something goes wrong.
- ☐ Characters get hurt.

What are some of the things you can do if you notice a person doing something that you think may be a **Pink Flag?**

- ☐ Ask a trusted adult for advice.
- ☐ If you feel safe, ask the person about the Pink Flag.
- ☐ Distance yourself from that person.

> **Snail Trail...**
> Cathy and Kyle are friends. Cathy had a large bag of chips and Kyle asked for some because he was hungry. Cathy didn't want to share, and although Kyle explained that he was hungry and that he would replace the chips later, Cathy refused to share. Cathy had refused to share many things with Kyle.

Snail Talk

Cathy's action is a **Pink Flag.** It shows that she may be losing interest in being Kyle's friend or that Kyle's hunger is not important to her. Taking care of your friend's needs when it is safe for you is a great way to build **Healthy Relationships**.

When you don't take care of your friend's needs or he/she doesn't take care of yours, it shows that you may not truly be friends. A true friend is always thinking about safety and what is best for his/her friend and their relationship. Kyle should pay attention to the **Pink Flag** and investigate further. He can tell Cathy about how this made him feel, and they should talk about Cathy's reasons for not sharing her chips and other things in general.

Activity

Identifying the Pink Flags

> **Snail Trail...**
> Abbie's friend Margaret shared that she posts her phone number on Social Media so that if boys like her they can get in touch with her easily. Abbie feels uneasy and is not sure why.

What could go wrong if you post your phone number on Social Media?

- [ ] Someone you don't know might call you.

- [ ] Someone you don't know might prank call you.

- [ ] Someone that you might not want to have your number will.

We would caution Margaret from posting her phone number so that random people can call her. Remember, safety is your first priority and relationships are built slowly and over time. Strangers should not have Margaret's phone number.

What should you do if your friend is doing something that causes you to feel uncomfortable?

☐ Tell him/her.

☐ Distance yourself.

☐ Discuss it with a trusted adult.

Snail Trail…

Katie notices that John is always lying to his mom and friends regarding his whereabouts. John also lies and makes excuses for not fulfilling his commitments. Most recently, Katie learns that John has figured out a way to take candy from the local grocery store without anyone noticing.

What are the **Pink Flags** in this situation?

_____
_____

What could happen in Katie and John's relationship if the **Pink Flags** are ignored?

_____
_____

🐌 **Snail talk**

Lying to your family and friends and stealing from a store are **Pink Flags** and may even become **Red Flags**. When John lies or steals, he demonstrates that he has no respect for his family/friends, for rules, or for other people's property. Stealing is illegal, and John could end up in jail. If Katie ignores these behaviors, John may also lie and steal from her.

Snail Trail…

Jose and Maria had known one another for several months. They are building a friendship. Unfortunately, Maria would cancel plans at the last minute.

Identify the **Pink Flag**:

_____

_____

_____

🐌 Snail Talk

Jose looked forward to seeing Maria, and because she cancelled at the last minute, he felt hurt and ignored. If someone cancels plans at the last minute for a good reason then you may be disappointed, but try to understand. Be polite and reschedule your plans with them.

However, if someone cancels often you need to ask, "What is going on, and is this a pattern?" This is a **Pink Flag** because it is not respectful to make plans with someone and then cancel at the last minute without good reason.

When you say you are going to do something you need to follow through, otherwise you will be thought of as unreliable. It is difficult to build a trusting relationship with someone who is unreliable.

🐌 Snail Wisdom

Pink Flags shouldn't be overlooked but instead they need to be discussed respectfully, openly, and honestly with your friend or dating partner. If you feel uncomfortable with something a person has said or done, then you have to check it out. It is always a good idea to talk with your parent/guardian or a trusted adult about Pink Flags.

> **Snail Trail...**
> Everett was waiting on campus for a class to start. A person who he didn't know came up to him and asked his name, phone number, and address. Everett gave the person the information that was requested.

Identify the **Pink Flags**:

_____

_____

 Snail Talk

NEVER give your personal information to someone that you don't know. Instead, be polite and let the person know that you are not comfortable giving that kind of information out to people you don't know.

> **Snail Trail...**
> Betty was on a first date with Jacob who she knew from a community activity. Jacob had invited Betty out to the movies. In order to maintain her safety, Betty decided to meet Jacob at the movie theatre. Once in the movies, Betty found the movie offensive and against her values because there was a great deal of sex and violence in the movie. She was feeling uncomfortable.

What would you do if you were Betty?

_____

_____

What would you do if you were Jacob and noticed that your date was uncomfortable at the movie?

_____

_____

 Snail Talk

Betty can do several things. She can tell Jacob that she is uncomfortable and ask to leave or go to another movie. If she is uncomfortable talking to Jacob, she can tell Jacob that she is going to the bathroom. Once in the bathroom, Betty can call her parents/guardian and ask to be picked up. She can then tell Jacob that her family had called while she was in the bathroom and that she needs to go home. If Jacob does not see Betty's side and gets angry, this can clearly be a **Pink Flag.**

Jacob could have discussed what movies were of interest with Betty. In the future, Betty and Jacob need to decide together on a movie that they can both enjoy.

Snail Wisdom

Always have an exit plan worked out in advance so that if you find yourself in an uncomfortable situation, you know what to do. Think about your exit plan like a fire drill. We practice drills so that we know what to do if there is an emergency. If you are on a date always have a parent/guardian or friend call you to make sure that you are safe at set times during the date. Develop a secret word or phrase that you can use if you are feeling unsafe; something simple like "How is grandma?" Remember to practice your exit plan.

> **Snail Trail...**
> Louissa and Ben have been dating on and off since high school. Ben is interested in a relationship with Louissa but not one that moves too quickly. He only wants to hold hands. He doesn't want to kiss.
>
> After dating for three months, Louissa wants to kiss. Ben is uncomfortable.

What should Ben do? Is this a **Pink Flag**?

_____

_____

_____

Snail Talk

Ben is not comfortable with kissing and he had already told Louissa. This is a **Pink Flag** because Louissa is not respecting Ben's wishes. People should only do what they are comfortable doing.

Activity

Kissing

What do you do when your date wants to kiss and you don't? Remember, building a Healthy Relationship takes time! If you are dating someone do not rush into a physical relationship. Do only what you are comfortable with and feel safe doing.

How will you share what you are comfortable doing with your date?

☐ Develop and agree on rules.

☐ Openly and honestly.

Write a list of what you are comfortable doing in a dating relationship:

_____

_____

Write a list of what you are NOT comfortable doing in a dating relationship:

_____

_____

What if you change your mind about something after you try it or you would like to try something after you have said that you didn't want to?

How will you tell someone that you changed your mind?

_____

_____

> **Snail Trail…**
>
> Rebecca has been friends with Martin on Social Media for over four months and they decide to meet at the mall. Martin is just an acquaintance to Rebecca. She has never met Martin in person before. The date is going well. Rebecca finds herself laughing with Martin and enjoying his company. Suddenly Martin announces that he would like to go to his car and get a sweatshirt. He wants Rebecca to go to the car with him.

Identify the **Pink Flags:**

_____

_____

Snail Talk

First of all, Rebecca has to maintain her safety. She really doesn't know Martin well since this is her first date. When Martin announces that he wants her to go to the car that can be a **Pink Flag**. Once at the car, anything can happen. Martin could force Rebecca to get into the car or he may behave in ways that could harm Rebecca. When Martin suggests that he and Rebecca go to his car, Rebecca can decide to be safe and stay behind. She can tell Martin that she will use the restroom while he is getting his sweatshirt. If he *insists* that she should go to the car with him, this is a **Pink Flag**; she should end the date. She can easily say, "Sorry, I can't go to the car with you, my parents/guardians are expecting me to stay in the mall."

Say this to yourself three times: **RELATIONSHIPS NEED TO BE SAFE. RELATIONSHIPS ARE BUILT SLOWLY AND OVER TIME.**

Activity

More Practice with Pink Flags

Think about the following Snail Trails select those that are appropriate. You can complete this activity with a partner and together discuss how you would handle the situation.

Snail Trail…

You are driving yourself to school and on the way you run out of gas. After a short while, a truck pulls over behind you and the driver gets out and greets you to see if he can help. The truck driver offers to take you to a gas station. What should you do? What can go wrong if you go with the truck driver? What can be your exit plan?

Snail Trail…

You are at the school's library and someone is staring at you. You stare back and the person begins to speak with you. The person then asks you to join him/her for coffee across the campus. What should you do? What can go wrong if you go with this person? What can be your exit plan?

Snail Trail…

You have been attending college for more than a couple of weeks and have made some friends with your classmates. One of your classmates has invited you to his/her home. What should you do? What can go wrong if you go to your classmate's home? What can be your exit plan?

Snail Trail…

You are walking across campus and a person comes up to you, smiles and introduces him/herself. He/she shares that he/she may have met you before because you look familiar. He/she then tells you that they could use your help putting something in his/her car. What do you do? What can go wrong if you go to the car with him/her? What can be your exit plan?

Snail Trail…

You are waiting on campus for your class to start and a person comes up to you and asks you to lend him/her some money. What do you do? What can go wrong if you give them some money? How do you say, "No"?

Snail Trail…

You are at a party and someone offers you a mixed drink and a pill promising you that it will be a lot of fun. What should you do? What can go wrong if you if you accept the drink and the pill? How can you say, "No"? What can be your exit plan if you decide to leave?

Snail Trail…

You are at party and someone gets in your face and starts to push and shove you. What should you do? What can go wrong if you push back? What can be your exit plan?

Snail Trail…

You are driving with a friend and they are speeding and driving recklessly. What should you do? What can go wrong if you do nothing? What can be your exit plan?

Snail Trail…

You are with a friend and they decide to use drugs and want you to join them? What can you do? What can go wrong if you join them? How can you say, "No"? What can be your exit plan if you join them?

Snail Trail…

You are on your first date and he/she wants to kiss. How will you react? What will you say? What can go wrong if you are uncomfortable and agree to the kiss? How can you say, "No"? What can be your exit plan?

Snail Trail…

Your date/friend is making a big decision without discussing it with you first. What should you discuss with him/her?

Snail Trail…

You are out bowling with your date/friend and he/she grabs you and hurts you. What should you do? What can be your exit plan?

Snail Trail…

Your friend is spreading lies about you and other friends are telling you. What should you do?

Snail Trail…

You are at a party with a group of friends and although everyone is over twenty-one, there is a lot of alcohol and you are uncomfortable. What should you do? What can go wrong if you stay and do nothing? What can be your exit plan?

Snail Trail…

You are shopping at the mall with your friend and you notice that he/she has just slipped an item into his/her pocket without buying it first. What should you do? What can go wrong if you say and do nothing? What can be your exit plan?

Reflection

What have you learned about **Pink Flags** and **Red Flags**?

_____

_____

_____

_____

_____

_____

_____

_____

_____

What word or phrase will you agree on with your parent or guardian that can be used to signal him/her that you want to end your time with your date or friend unexpectedly?

_____

_____

_____

In order to protect your safety, you should always have an exit plan before you sense **Pink** and **Red Flags**. What is your safety plan?

_____

_____

_____

Chapter 3

Knowing What You Want

Attributes & Characteristics

Knowing What You Want

It is part of human nature to want an intimate and close relationship with someone. Sometimes we want a dating partner. Looking for a dating partner when you have not identified what it is that you want is like going to a grocery store without a shopping list.

This chapter is designed to help you sort through the features and characteristics that you may find appealing. The purpose is to help you narrow what it is that you are looking for in someone who will be special to you.

Before you start dating, you have to know what it is that you are looking for in a person and the relationship. Otherwise, you may end up with unwanted heartache, pain, and drama.

It can be helpful to consider answering a few questions before you even begin a dating relationship:

- Do I even want a relationship?
- Am I looking for social status, for others to think that I am cool because I am with someone?
- Am I looking for someone to put me on a pedestal and worship me by putting my needs ahead of his or her?
- Do I just want to get away from my family or friends?
- Am I looking for a sexual outlet?

What are you looking for?

_____

_____

_____

It is important to know what you are looking for in a dating relationship. Be willing to take your time and find someone who really cares about you and what you want.

Snail Talk

Building a **Healthy Relationship** is an investigative process that is built upon open and honest communication, shared respect, trust, and goals. We say "built" because it takes work. It is like creating a vegetable garden with another person. You both have to agree on the vegetables that you want to grow and decide what each of you will do to take care of the garden.

By discussing your shared goals and following through on what you each commit to, you will build mutual trust and respect for each other and the relationship. To create a good garden, you have to communicate well. You have to talk about what is working and what needs to be done to make things better. You each have to be open to the feedback and be willing to make changes that will help you both create a good garden.

Snail Wisdom

Meaningful relationships can develop when you like someone and they like you back the same way.

List what you want from a relationship?

_____

_____

Why do you think that you are ready to date?

_____

_____

_____

The first step to finding someone is to decide what type of person you are looking for and figure out what type of physical features that you're attracted to the most.

You can begin with thinking about the physical features and general characteristics. What type of features and general characteristics do you find most pleasing?

_____

_____

_____

> **Snail Trail…**
>
> The characteristics that Tara listed for a date included someone to keep her secrets, someone who was romantic, nice and polite, and Japanese. She loves anime and believes that all Japanese men like anime as well. Her plan was to move to Japan from the USA to find a husband.

 Snail Talk

Tara loves anime and it is only for this reason she sees herself living in Japan with a Japanese husband. Tara should be more realistic. She does not speak Japanese and is very close to her family. She can consider adjusting her list to include finding someone who shares the same interests in anime. By doing so, she opens herself to anyone who likes anime and may be able to find that person without having to move abroad.

List some of your interests:

_____

_____

_____

_____

_____

_____

Being realistic means setting goals that are doable. Try not to have goals that are difficult or impossible to achieve because these types of goals only lead to disappointment.

List some of your goals:

_____

_____

_____

_____

_____

_____

Attributes & Characteristics

In the following pages you will find lists of physical features and attributes to help you identify what you are looking for and are attracted to.

Physical features: Check the boxes that interest you.

Height	Tall	Average	Short
Weight	Heavy	Average	Thin
Hair Color	Dark	Medium	Light
Eye Color	Blue	Brown	Variation
Hair Length	Long	Medium	Short
Hair Type	Coarse	Curly	Straight
Teeth	Straight and very white	Average	Unimportant
Smile	Always	Sometimes	Hardly ever
Handsome or Pretty	Model perfect	Average	Unimportant
Athletic	Very	Somewhat	Unimportant
Age	Older	The same	Younger

Look at the boxes that you've checked for physical features and write out your list. I would like someone who looks like...

Physical Features	Your Answers
1. Height	
2. Weight	
3. Hair color	
4. Eye color	
5. Teeth	
6. Smile	
7. Other qualities	

Examples:

Race/nationality

Religion

Attributes & Characteristics: Check the boxes that interest you.

Highly intelligent	Very smart	Smart
Extremely witty	Funny	Serious
Highly logical	Very logical	Logical
Very sensitive	Sensitive	Somewhat sensitive
Outgoing with high energy	Friendly energetic	Shy and reserved
Accepting and supportive of others	Moderate acceptance/supportive of others	Challenging/ difficult to get along with
Extremely respectful of family and society	Respectful of family and society	Doesn't care or ignores family and society
Extremely kind	Kind only if it serves his/her purpose	Confrontational/harsh approach
Extremely interested in you	Balanced interest in you and themselves	Self centered
Good listener/validating	Listens but doesn't always validate	Not interested in listening, more interested in getting their point across

Attributes & Characteristics: Check the boxes that interest you.

Accommodating & tolerant	Moderately agreeable & tolerant	Likes to win/control outcomes, low/no tolerance
Thoughtful and considerate/ able to anticipate needs of others	Thoughtful at times and over time learns from experience	Focused on own needs
Slowly investigates relationship	Moderate speed	Very quick development
Very honest and open	Honest	Guarded and secretive
Very hard worker	Good worker	Okay worker
Extremely attentive	Very attentive	Somewhat Attentive
Very Spiritual/Religious	Spiritual/religious	Not religious
Very family orientated	Family oriented	Not family orientated
Believes in joint decision making	Can make independent and joint decisions	Independent decision maker

Attributes & Characteristics: Check the boxes that interest you.

Very generous with time and money	Moderately generous with time and money	Frugal with time and money
High public displays of affection/romantic	Medium public displays of affection	Low public displays of affection
Collaborative	Average competitive	Highly competitive
Aggressive	Assertive	Compliant
Highly creative	Somewhat creative	Not important
Loves pets	Good with pets	Neutral
Likes to be prepared in advance, reliable and punctual	Reliable and punctual	Distracted and needs reminders

Congratulations! You've just described the type of person that interests you. You have identified the main qualities of a person to whom you may be attracted.

Remember that dating and building **Healthy Relationships** is an investigative process that takes time and effort, so feel free to update your list as you investigate.

Snail Trail...

Dan and Lisa believed that they were ready to start a dating relationship. Dan had some features on his list that Lisa didn't have. At first, Dan was concerned because Lisa didn't fit his top features: blonde hair and blue eyes. He thought that the relationship might not work because Lisa had brown hair and brown eyes.

 Snail Talk

After getting to know Lisa, Dan realized that the most important things to him were honesty, willingness to do activities, and cheerfulness. These things were clearly part of Lisa's personality. These qualities were more important than someone who had blonde hair and blue eyes. Dan found that he liked Lisa because of who she was and her honesty and positive outlook on life were very attractive to him.

List what is important to you. For instance, the following list may contain things that you have learned from your parents and guardians that might have been referred to as things they valued: telling the truth, not stealing, being on time. Think about how these values (items) might be more important than the physical features that you have chosen and write your list of values (things that are important to you):

_____

_____

_____

_____

_____

_____

_____

_____

Chapter 4

Wash it, Brush it, and Tuck it

Levels of Personal Hygiene

Wash it, Brush it, and Tuck it

Relationships and friendships create love and affection between people. It is difficult to care for and love someone else if you don't care for and love yourself. Self-love begins with self-care and grooming. People notice and are typically attracted to one another through their five senses (sight, sound, touch, taste, and smell). What a person looks like and smells like when you interact with them matters.

How his or her voice sounds when they speak and how they feel, when touched, are all parts of what makes them attractive. Good personal hygiene is paying attention to yourself and making sure that you are at your best in all these categories. Personal hygiene and grooming are extremely important because they tell the world so much about you. When you ignore them, you are telling others that you do not care for yourself. How will you care for another if you are not caring for yourself?

Snail Wisdom

Remember you rarely get a second chance to make that first impression.

Everyone has heard of the great love story of Romeo and Juliet. Romeo first sees Juliet at her family's party. He notices her beauty and can't take his eyes off of her. Next, she notices him looking at her and she can't take her eyes off of him. Think how they would feel about each other if either had dirty hair, rotten teeth, and smelled of body odor. If they didn't find each other attractive, they would not have begun the investigation that lead to their relationship. The initial attraction that Romeo and Juliet felt was clearly based upon physical attraction.

Activity

Loving yourself is about the relationship that you have with yourself

Most of us use mirrors to see if we look good. For the most part, we are looking to see if our reflection matches how we physically want to look. Our goal is to make sure that our articles of clothing match, our hair is combed, and we are presentable. The purpose of spending time in front of the mirror is to make sure that others see us positively. We typically do not look at our reflection admiringly or lovingly and we don't look for what is right about us.

Let's look in the mirror for our real self.

1. Stand in front of a mirror and take a good look at yourself.

2. What is your self talk? These are the things that you think and tell yourself about yourself.

What are you saying to yourself about yourself?

_____

_____

Is what you are saying to yourself positive? List these things:

_____

_____

If it is negative, where have you heard it before and what changes do you want to make? List these things:

_____

_____

Have you taken good care of yourself? List the things that show that you have:

_____

_____

Learn to give and accept compliments. Express love for yourself and others willingly, and often.

> **Snail Trail…**
>
> Maritza decided that she was ready to date because she had just had a birthday and got new clothing. She spent time getting her hair straightened. She looked truly amazing and was beginning to get the attention that she was hoping for. However, Maritza didn't brush and floss her teeth often. She didn't understand why people stepped slightly away when she tried to talk with them.

Think about what could be wrong with Maritza and write your ideas here:

_____

_____

What should you do daily to care for yourself? How do you get ready in the morning? Does your routine show that you care for yourself?

_____

_____

Why is it important to look your best?

- [ ] So, people will know that you care about yourself.

- [ ] First impressions are lasting impressions.

- [ ] So, that people will want to get to know you.

- [ ] So, you are not offensive and turn people off.

What types of things could you do to make sure that you always look your best?

_____

_____

How can you tell when people are not taking good care of themselves?

- [ ] Their clothes are wrinkled and dirty.

- [ ] Their teeth haven't been brushed.

- [ ] Their hair is dirty and uncombed.

- [ ] They have bad odor.

Levels of Personal Hygiene

There are three levels of personal hygiene and self care. Check the box where you are most comfortable.

☐ **Just get up and go**: This person looks like he or she just got out of bed. He/she appears messy. His/her hair is not combed, the clothes look like they have been worn several days in a row, and he/she does not smell fresh. There is dirt under his/her fingernails, and toenails and he/she does not trim them regularly. When you look closely, he/she may have plaque build-up on his/her teeth, and his/her gums may be red and swollen. He/she looks like he/she needs a shower and, more importantly, he/she appears as if no one loves him/her!

☐ **I'll make an effort if I have to**: This person knows how to put him/her self together with clothing and accessories but isn't committed to doing so for every day styling. He/she generally is clean and groomed, but can go through periods when he/she doesn't care as much. He/she can dress neatly but he/she may only really dress up well for special occasions.

☐ **I enjoy looking my best**: This person knows how to put his or herself together with clothing and accessories and does so daily. He/she tends to dress nicely and enjoys the special attention and compliments that others pay him/her routinely. This person makes an effort to pay special attention to his/her health and grooming. His/her hair is always clean, combed, and cut well. His/her teeth and nails are well taken care of. He/she wears clean clothes and he/she smells fresh. In fact, he or she may look as if always dressed for a special occasion to the average person.

Did you know that the colors you choose to wear can create feelings in others? Pay attention to the colors you select for different occasions. Reds, yellows, and oranges may seem to be warm and stimulating; however, they may also indicate over confidence or be perceived as too bold. Blues, greens, and neutrals such as grays and browns are good choices because they tend to bring on feelings of peace, calm, and serenity.

List your favorite colors:

_____

_____

What do you think your favorite colors communicate to others?

_____

_____

Check your favorite colors:

Red	Blue	Green	Yellow
Pink	Blue purple	Blue green	Yellow orange
Red orange	Purple	Forrest green	Sunshine yellow
Orange	Red purple	Lime green	Yellow green

Check what you think your favorite colors communicate to others:

Red	**Blue**	**Green**	**Yellow**
Energy	Peace	Growth	Joy
Strength	Calm	Freshness	Happiness
Power	Loyalty	Safety	Wisdom

Snail Wisdom

Your sense of smell has the strongest ability to help you remember. Generally males prefer scents that remind them of home, with vanilla being the most popular familiar scent. Girls on the other hand tend to prefer floral and fruitier scents.

List your top three favorite smells. What do they remind you of?

_____

_____

_____

Your teeth, gums, and how well you take care of them are a part of your smile. Your oral health will also impact your overall well being. Your oral hygiene can attract or turn off people that you communicate with.

- Do you get regular dental check-ups? Yes or No
- How often do you brush your teeth? _____
- When was the last time you got a new tooth brush? _____
(Toothbrushes should be replaced every 3-4 months.)
- How often do you floss? _____
- How often do you shower? _____
- How often do you wash your hair? _____
- Do you wear deodorant? _____ How often? _____

If you are not brushing your teeth and showering daily, you, your health, and your friend and dating prospects are at great risk. Contact your dentist for recommendations for proper care of your teeth, your gums, and your breath.

Snail Talk

Being clean and looking your best shows that you care for yourself and others. Also remember you may be clean, but if your clothes are dirty, torn, wrinkled, or ill-fitting, with buttons missing or are not tucked in, you probably don't look your best. Your clothing should fit you correctly.

What does your overall appearance tell the world about you?

_____

_____

- Ask your best friend to list the ways that you could improve your personal hygiene.
- Ask your best friend to list the ways that you could improve your appearance.

Snail Trail…

Luke and his friend Sal shared a tuna fish sandwich during lunch. Luke ran into Tracy, the girl he has had a crush on, and he reached out to hug her. She pulled away, and he was offended.

What could have caused Tracy's reaction?

☐ Luke had tuna breathe.

☐ Luke may have surprised Tracy wanting to hug.

☐ Luke may have had sandwich in his teeth and on his face.

What could Luke have done differently?

_____
_____
_____

Snail Wisdom

Looking good is not just about having new clothes or wearing the latest fashion fads. It's about taking pride in the way you look. Showering daily, wearing deodorant, and attending to your personal grooming needs are keys to successful interactions with others.

Summarize what good hygiene means to you:

_____
_____
_____
_____
_____
_____
_____

Chapter 5

Meeting Someone New

Enjoying One Another's Company

Meeting Someone New

Everyone needs a friend, and at some point many people would like to develop an even closer relationship with a person. Developing friendships with people can be difficult and time consuming. There are skills that can be learned to help avoid drama and pain. In this chapter you will learn about yourself and how to create and maintain a **Healthy Relationship**.

Let's begin…

You have begun to notice someone in whom you are interested. Maybe you have always noticed that interesting person but didn't know how to handle your feelings for him/her.

You may even be able to spot that special someone in a crowd. Maybe you have even checked online sites to answer questions like: *How to make friends?* or, *How to get a date?* Or you may have asked your parents and your best friends what you should say, do, and be like in relationships.

Developing a friendship and dating someone takes time and hard work. Most people look for someone to be attracted to while hoping that this person will be their friend or fall in love with them. Their dream is to be with someone who wants to make them happy.

Building **Healthy Relationships** with someone takes honest communication. Both people must work hard to create and keep trust, and respect, and to share their intentions. We all get hurt when trust is broken, respect for someone, when we want different things. More importantly, we get hurt when we stop communicating well.

Activity

Honest Communication

The following questions are designed to help you think about what it feels like to be honest. The responses to the questions are your own and don't need to be shared with others.

If you had to share a secret with your parent/guardian or friend, what would you share? Write down the secret that you would tell:

_____

_____

_____

Think about a time when you did something that made you feel uncomfortable and you had to share it, even though you knew that you might get into trouble or feel embarrassed. What could the other person have done to make it easier for you to share your story?

_____

_____

Remember a time when someone did something nice for you. Did you respond by saying thank you? Think about something that someone has done that worked out well for you and share how what they did made you feel deep down inside:

_____

_____

Always remember that communicating honestly is the willingness to share what you are really thinking and feeling openly, respectfully, and truthfully with the person. Think about what is important for someone special to know about you and write a list:

_____

_____

You'll need more than chance and good fortune to make a **Healthy Relationship** work. You have to first know yourself and then be willing to share this information with someone special. You must also be willing to learn about the other person and be willing to talk honestly to each other in order to make the relationship work.

For some people it takes a lifetime to get it right. What you want is a relationship that makes you feel happier and better than the way you were when you were single.

Remember, figuring out what you really want in a relationship is the first step. Here are some questions to consider again:

- Are you looking for someone just to be with while at school or in the community?
- Are you looking for someone that you also do things with on the weekends?
- Are you looking to build a long-term friendship with someone?
- Are you looking for someone to date?
- Are you looking for someone to date seriously and for a long time?

Snail Wisdom

By listening to the things that people say you need to change about yourself, you'll be able to discover the patterns and themes that may be keeping you from being successful in relationships. Feedback is a gift that you can use to improve yourself or to continue doing what you are doing well.

Activity

Exploring what you want

Do you know what you are looking for in a relationship? Knowing your needs and expectations before you go looking for the other person will help you be more successful.

Consider the following:

Are you looking for someone just to be with while at school or in the community? When do you plan on getting together with this person?

- [ ] In the evening.
- [ ] During a lunch break.
- [ ] After school/work.

Are you looking for someone that you also do things with on the weekends? How do you plan on arranging weekend events?

_____

_____

_____

Are you looking to build a long-term friendship with someone? Why would someone want to be your friend?

_____

_____

_____

Are you looking for someone to date? What is it that you want from a dating relationship?

_____

_____

_____

Are you looking for someone to date seriously and for a long time? List the ways you would like to be treated by this person:

_____

_____

_____

Let's review…

Building **Healthy Relationships** is like going on a learning field trip that involves two people who are curious about themselves and each other.

Through spending time with each other and sharing information, a couple can build a friendship first and then decide if they want to invest more in the relationship.

As you each communicate your needs and discuss and meet each other's expectations, you begin to trust and respect each other as you work towards your shared goals.

Enjoying One Another's Company

Different social settings provide you with the opportunity to see the other person and your relationship with him/her in different ways. For example, you may find out that your friend is very open and talkative when he/she is alone with you, but when interacting with your family, he/she becomes very quiet and shy. Discovering this information about a person is all part of investigating the relationship. Next you will find some activities that will help you manage your social interactions with the other person.

Activity
Inviting your friend/date to your home

There are several reasons for inviting someone to your home. The main reason is that you want this person to meet your family and see where you live. Another reason is to see what your family and other friends think about the new person in your life and how they all get along with one another. The benefit of doing this is that once your family meets and approves of this person, you can then rely on their support of the relationship. Your family can also help you arrange opportunities to get together with this person. We recommend that the first time you have this person over it should be to socialize with you and your family. You may play a board game, watch a movie or share a meal. This will allow for everyone to get to know each other.

 Snail Wisdom

When you are invited to someone's home, it is always a wonderful gesture to bring a treat such as flowers, dessert, or other food items to show appreciation for the invitation.

Planning ahead and identifying the needs you both have can help to ensure an enjoyable time together. We have created 4 check lists to help you plan the most common activities that people typically enjoy sharing. You can apply the steps in each list to other activities as well. Place a check in the box provided as you plan. Each item checked is worth one point. Add your total points at the end to see how you did.

When inviting someone to your home, consider the following:

- [ ] Discuss the invitation with your parents/guardians, siblings, roommates.
- [ ] Think about: activities, games, meals, movies, etc; that your guest may enjoy with your parents/guardians, siblings, roommates.
- [ ] Discuss the invitation/ideas with the person that you would like to invite and get his/her approval.
- [ ] Agree on a date.
- [ ] Agree on a beginning time.
- [ ] Agree on an ending time.
- [ ] Share your address.
- [ ] Help prepare for the event.
- [ ] Total: If you have earned 8 points you have prepared well.

List the things that you'll need to have prior to your guest's arrival:

_____

_____

A popular choice for many people is to go out to the movies. It is very important to discuss what movie you'll be seeing with your friend/date. This is a sure way to avoid feeling awkward or uncomfortable when viewing movies. Reading the movie reviews can also help to determine which movie is best. Place a check in the box provided as you plan. Each item checked is worth one point. Add your total points at the end to see how you did.

Things to do prior to attending a movie with a friend or a date:

- [ ] Find out what is playing at the local theater and make a list of the movies that seem interesting.
- [ ] Read reviews and ratings about the movies of interest online.
- [ ] Narrow your movies of interest to two or three and note the times, the lengths, and the ratings of each of the movies.
- [ ] Discuss the details of the movies with your friend/date and get their opinion on which movie he/she would like to see.
- [ ] Agree on the movie of interest.
- [ ] Discuss how you and your friend will get to the theater and how he/she will get home.

- [ ] Agree on who will pay: pay for your own, take turns, or treat.
- [ ] Discuss extra money needed for drink and food items.
- [ ] Total: If you have earned 8 points, you have prepared well.

What types of movies do you like: dramas, comedies, action, cartoon, animation, etc.?

_____

_____

Attending a bowling alley, miniature golf course or other outing is a great way to get to know your friend's/date's interests and learn more about him/her. Place a check in the box provided as you plan. Each item checked is worth one point. Add your total points at the end to see how you did.

Things to do prior to going bowling, miniature golfing or other activity:

- [ ] Call the place of interest and ask for the hours of operation and the best times and days to attend. This may help you to avoid crowds and long waiting times.
- [ ] Discuss the place, times, and days with your friend/date.
- [ ] Agree on the place, set a time, and consider how long you expect to be doing the activity.
- [ ] Discuss items that you will need to take with you. For bowling you will need money for shoe rental or if you own bowling shoes and ball, socks, etc. You'll need to remember to pack these things.
- [ ] Agree on how you will get to the activity.
- [ ] Agree on how you will pay: pay for your own, take turns or treat.
- [ ] Discuss other monies needed for snacks, game machines and other items.
- [ ] Total: If you have earned 7 points, you have prepared well.

Think about what is needed to participate in the activity and what you might need. It is also nice to anticipate the needs of your guest.

List the types of things you need to plan for with your friend/date to participate in the activity:

_____

_____

Attending community functions are fun and easy ways to see how the other person behaves socially: dances, proms, bingo, gyms, etc. What activities would you like to do with your friend/date?

_____

_____

What do you enjoy doing? What functions are available to you in your community? If you don't know you can call your local community center, religious institutions, and libraries. You can also look in your local newspaper to get information on community clubs and activities:

_____

_____

Dining out is a wonderful way to learn more about your friend/date. Place a check in the box provided as you plan your outing. Each item checked is worth one point. Add your total points at the end to see how you did.

Things to do prior to going to a restaurant:

- [ ] Visit the restaurant of interest on line or in person if you are not familiar with it and its menu.
- [ ] Review the menu to see if you like the food that they serve. Be sure to discuss any dietary limitations.
- [ ] For the more expensive restaurants call and find out if a reservation is recommended. Find out about how long it typically takes to eat from appetizer through dessert.
- [ ] Share this information with your friend/date.
- [ ] Agree on the restaurant, the time, and day.
- [ ] Agree on how you will pay the bill: split, take turns, or treat.
- [ ] Discuss how you will get to the restaurant and how long you intend on being there.
- [ ] Total: If you have earned 7 points, you have prepared well.

List the restaurants that you'd be interested in and their food choices:

_____

_____

_____

Meeting people that you share things in common with can be challenging. For some, it is never easy to communicate the desire to create a friendship or dating relationship. However, what we know is that everyone wants a friend/date, and sometimes you need to just take a chance by attending an event or joining a class. Always remember the lessons that you have already learned about looking for **Pink Flags** and investigating relationships over time.

Once you think that you're ready for the responsibility of dating, there are many ways to let the person you like know, but remember:

- Don't be pushy.

- "No" means "No."

- Don't burn bridges; you may need this relationship in the future. Clearly, this means if you burn the bridge you will not be able to walk across it in the future. Similarly, if you make people angry they will be unwilling to help you in the future.

Once you have found someone with whom you are interested in developing a friendship or dating relationship with, you have two options:

1. **Ask a friend to approach the person of interest on your behalf.**
This is the most popular approach, because neither you, nor the other person, have to deal with asking and hearing a "No". This makes saying "No" and hearing "No" easier.

2. **You can talk to the person you like directly.**
This can be awkward, but remember that the worst thing that can happen is to hear that they don't want to get to know you. This simply means that the person is saying "No" to the relationship and is not saying "No" to you as a person.

Snail Talk

Just remember, if someone asks you to be his/her friend or date and you are not interested, thank them for liking you and for asking. Then as kindly as you can, say that you are not available or interested. You can do the same thing if someone approached you on his/her friend's behalf.

Always ask, is this person safe for me to develop a friendship with or to date?

If you decide that you want to date, you should be dating someone close to your age group and not someone who is a lot older or a lot younger. Sometimes older people have crushes on younger people, and vice-versa. Always check with a parent or guardian if you are unsure.

It is easier to meet people with similar interests through school clubs, religious groups, and other activities. Putting yourself out there to meet and spend time with people you know nothing about can be difficult.

Activity

Meeting new people

Meeting through family and friends:

Ask a friend or family member if he/she knows someone who is interested in having a relationship. This could be a brother, sister, relative, or a friend that might be interested in meeting someone.

Meeting for Common Interest/Community Events:

Read your local newspaper to determine a schedule of events that might be of interest to you and record the schedule on the lines provided.

- [ ] Dances _____
- [ ] Plays _____
- [ ] Bowling _____
- [ ] Coffee shops _____
- [ ] Library events _____
- [ ] Other _____

Meeting through local clubs:

- [ ] Gym _____
- [ ] Lions Club _____
- [ ] Kiwanis _____
- [ ] Garden _____
- [ ] Other _____

Meeting through volunteering:

☐ Non profit _____

☐ Library _____

☐ Community center _____

☐ School _____

☐ Other _____

Meeting through classes:

☐ Art _____

☐ Cooking _____

☐ Reading _____

☐ Computers _____

☐ Other _____

Make a list of other places where you can meet new people.

_____

_____

_____

_____

_____

_____

Activity

Acquaintance to Friendship

Joe and Lisa met at the bowling alley. Joe decided that he really wanted to get to know Lisa better.

What strategy did Joe use?

_____

_____

_____

How did Joe maintain his safety as he investigated his relationship with Lisa further?

☐ Kept the meetings with Lisa in a public place.

☐ Other people would be around on the bowling team, so Joe wasn't alone.

☐ Friends and guardians knew Joe was bowling.

Meeting through Social Media

Always remember that your safety is your first priority. If you choose to meet someone that you have been in contact with through Social Media, always meet in a public place, tell your parent/guardian where you are going, and bring along a friend/parent/guardian. Anyone you meet through Social Media is a stranger. It is very easy for the person that you are in communication with to lie about his/her identity and intentions.

Social networking sites are now more popular than ever before. Meeting new people online has become more acceptable and for many, it is easier to meet someone online than in person because there isn't a lot of risk with meeting someone at a distance.

However, it is also a lot easier for someone who is online to fool someone and create a false identity to attract people into relationships. So in order to protect your safety, you need to become knowledgeable, question what you are told, and check out what you think might be true.

Snail Wisdom

Think before you post. You are responsible for your words and, more often than not, technology lives on forever. What you put on the web stays on the web for everyone to see. So if you regret your post, you are stuck with it.

Let's review…

1. Make sure that the facts that you are given online match the story you are told.

2. Do a background check on the person with whom you are interacting online. Ask questions and seek the opinion and advice of friends/parents/guardians.

3. Think about the information that you communicate about yourself online. Do not provide private information (such as your address, birth date, social security number, living circumstances, family particulars, etc.)

4. Avoid posting information about yourself that can potentially cause you harm.

5. Never meet up alone with the person you've met online. Always bring a friend or family member and meet in a public place.

6. Never send sexually explicit material electronically. If you receive such materials seek the advice of a trusted adult.

Snail Talk

Employers often look online to learn about applicants. So if you have posted inappropriate photographs or information about yourself online, it can hurt your reputation and your chance of being considered for employment.

Meeting in Person

When you meet someone you like remember to use conversation to help find out about each other. Having a conversation is like building a structure with blocks. The goal is to gather and share enough information to build a better understanding of each other and to keep each other interested as the relationship develops. People enjoy spending time with someone who is able to make them feel good about themselves. People do this mutually by showing an interest in what the other person is saying. Each person has their own blocks of information and together he/she takes turns sharing and building the structure.

One partner places a block and the next partner thinks about where to place his or her block in order to continue the conversation. We use conversation to determine if we have things in common with others and to decide if we want to have a relationship and become friends. The more people have in common with each other and the more their differences compliment each other, the more time each person wants to spend with the other. As you talk, you can build on what your partner is sharing or you can add a new topic. Some people find it difficult to carry a conversation. Here are some helpful tips:

- Remember that you communicate with your words as well as with your body. So positioning your body in a relaxed and open posture shows that you are interested in the other person and the conversation. Looking at the other person; and nodding your head in agreement while the person speaks shows that you are interested and are hearing what is being said.

- Remember that people typically like to talk about themselves, so look for ways to get others to share information about who they are and their experiences.

- Do not hog the conversation. Remember that everyone likes a good listener. Instead look for natural pauses in the conversation to share information about yourself.

Activity

Building Conversations

You may ask, have you always lived here? What do you like the most and the least about living here? You can look for something that you find interesting about the other person and ask them about it.

For example: That is a very interesting bag. Where did you get it?

You can ask someone if they can recommend a local restaurant, store, etc.

You can ask about a person's job, school, family, hobbies, or pets.

List some questions that you may want to ask a person on your first meeting that will tell you some things about who they are:

_____

_____

To listen effectively, when the person responds to your questions, select something from what they shared with you and ask another question based on one thing that they shared. This is how you pass information back and forth, just like when you are playing tennis and are passing the ball.

For example: You can ask someone to tell you about his/her family. They can respond by saying "I come from a **family of five** and **we live in town**."

In this scenario, you can then ask, "**How many brothers and sisters** do you have or **what do you like about living in town**?" Then you can share information about yourself if no questions are asked of you.

In this scenario, the person responded with two things that you could easily build on by asking another question about what you heard. The information you gather in a conversation will help you find out if you share any interests with the other person, and you will also get clues about whether or not this person wants to build a relationship with you. As the two people work on communicating, they can move toward a friendship or begin dating.

Here are some conversation categories and the corresponding questions you can ask to help you meet and learn about someone. Make sure you listen to the other person's answers and remember their response for future conversations. Remember what the other person shared and refer to the information in future conversations. This shows the other person that you listened and cared about what they were talking about.

Family

How many siblings do you have?

If you asked someone this question and he/she responded: "I have two siblings." What question could you ask next or what statement about your life could you share by building on their response?

For instance, you could say, "Who else lives in your home?" or "I have four people living in my home."

What question or statement are you thinking about?

_____

_____

What do your parents do?

If you asked someone this question and he/she responded: "My father is a builder and my mother is a teacher." What question could you ask next or what statement about your life could you share by building on their response?

_____

_____

What is the best thing about your family?

If you asked someone this question and he/she responded: "They always support me." What question could you ask next or what statement about your life could you share by building on their response?

_____

_____

What are some of the challenging things about your family?

If you asked someone this question and he/she responded: "My sister bothers me." What question could you ask next or what statement about your life could you share by building on their response?

_____

_____

What house rule do you like least?

If you asked someone this question and he/she responded: "I have to keep my room clean." What question could you ask next or what statement about your life could you share by building on their response?

_____

_____

Foods

What is your favorite food?

If you asked someone this question and he/she responded: "My favorite food is pizza." What question could you ask next or what statement about your life could you share by building on their response?

_____

_____

Do you know how to cook?

If you asked someone this question and he/she responded: "I like to make waffles." What question could you ask next or what statement about your life could you share by building on their response?

_____

_____

Do you have a favorite restaurant?

If you asked someone this question and he/she responded: "No." What question could you ask next or what statement about your life could you share by building on their response?

_____

_____

Pets

Do you have any pets?

If you asked someone this question and he/she responded: "I have a dog and two cats." What question could you ask next or what statement about your life could you share by building on their response?

_____

_____

What is your favorite animal?

If you asked someone this question and he/she responded: "I love lions."

What question could you ask next or what statement about your life could you share by building on their response?

___

___

If you could own any animal what would it be?

If you asked someone this question and he/she responded: "I would like to have a monkey." What question could you ask next or what statement about your life could you share by building on their response?

___

___

Work

Where would you like to work?

If you asked someone this question and he/she responded: "I would like to work in a pet store." What question could you ask next or what statement about your life could you share by building on their response?

___

___

Interests

What do you do for fun?

If you asked someone this question and he/she responded: "I play video games." What question could you ask next or what statement about your life could you share by building on their response?

___

___

What is your favorite color?

If you asked someone this question and he/she responded: "Red."

What question could you ask next or what statement about your life could you share by building on their response?

_____

_____

Do you have a best friend?

If you asked someone this question and he/she responded: "My brother is my best friend." What question could you ask next or what statement about your life could you share by building on their response?

_____

_____

What is your favorite movie?

If you asked someone this question and he/she responded: "I like all of the James Bond movies." What question could you ask next or what statement about your life could you share by building on their response?

_____

_____

Fun hobbies

Do you collect anything and if so what do you collect?

If you asked someone this question and he/she responded: "I collect pennies."

What question could you ask next or what statement about your life could you share by building on their response?

_____

_____

Let's review…

You have agreed to meet someone that you would like to get to know:

- Always keep your safety in mind, so ask to meet in a public place.

- If you have friends in common ask them what they can tell you about the person of interest.

- Tell your parent/guardian or friend what you are about to do, where you are going, and at what time to expect you home.

- Investigate this person by asking your questions. Develop some questions to ask this person about who he/she is and what he/she likes, or ask about his/her family, what the family does for fun, what work family members are involved with, what religion do they belong to, and other questions that will help you learn about this person.

- If you enjoyed meeting this person and you got along well, repeat the process and introduce this person to your friends and family.

- Always remember to meet in a public place until you and your family and friends all agree that this person is trustworthy and feels safe.

Snail Wisdom

You can bring a friend or family member along as you get to know someone that you do not know much about. Getting another's opinion about your date can help you decide if they are suitable and safe for you. If you like the person always remember relationships are built over time!

Meeting people who you don't know well or with whom you don't share friends can be dangerous. Remember SAFETY COMES FIRST.

Snail Trail…
Ashley was on a Social Media site when she "friended" a friend of a friend. She felt safe because the site provided her with an opportunity to become friends with Paul.

Snail Talk

Just because the site uses the name friend doesn't mean that you know this person. Remember this person is just an acquaintance. Be extremely careful on Social Media sites.

How can you protect yourself while you are online or are using Social Media sites?

- ☐ Don't share personal information.
- ☐ Investigate what the person is saying to make sure that it is true.
- ☐ Seek a trusted adult's opinion.

What are some of the things that can go wrong when interacting with people you have met on Social Media?

- ☐ He/she may not be who he/she says.
- ☐ He/she may want to take advantage of you.
- ☐ He/she may be looking to trick you into doing something you shouldn't.

Meeting a person for the first time:

It is important to always tell someone where, when, and with whom you'll be spending time. Plan a **"check in"** many times during the date with someone who cares about you. Always have an exit plan in mind. Remember, not everyone has the same intentions that you do.

There are many dangers when meeting people through the Internet. Sometimes people who we meet online aren't actually who they say they are. They may be older, and they may intend to harm you. Please be aware that there are predators who frequent these sites looking specifically for young people to take advantage of.

What can go wrong when meeting a person for the first time?

_____

_____

How will you protect yourself if you meet up with someone that you've spoken to through Social Media when none of your friends know this person?

_____

_____

Please remember that if an adult (anyone over the age of 18) is showing interest in a minor (someone under the age of 18) both people should think twice before moving forward and discuss it with a trusted adult, a counselor, or law enforcement officer. Here's a good rule: if it's illegal DON'T DO IT.

Chapter 6

Relationships Take Time

Shared Trust
Shared Respect
Effective Communication
Shared Goals
Becoming Friends

Relationships Take Time

As mentioned in previous chapters, relationships develop over time and they take work. Both friendships and dating relationships need to be investigated by the people involved. Together the people involved develop a set of relationship rules. In addition, because relationships take time there are stages that relationships move through as the people involved become closer. In this chapter we will look at what is needed for building **Healthy Relationships.**

Snail Wisdom

Building a Healthy Relationship is an investigative process. It is a relationship between two people who spend time with each other in different social settings. It's like going on a field trip; you decide where you want to go to, pack and prepare, and hope for an exciting journey as you stop along the way to see new things, refuel, or take a break.

In a Healthy Relationship you agree to share the expenses, responsibilities, and even the decision making. To have a good relationship, all parties must agree on what type of relationship is going to be formed with respect, trust, and good communication at all times.

Snail Talk

Any relationship, dating or not, improves when the parties agree to create and stick with a **Code of Conduct.** Think about the field trip analogy again. Before going on the field trip, everyone agrees about the route to take, what type of music to play and when and where to stop for food and rest.

In any video game, the **Code of Conduct** is stated in the rules for playing the game and typically the players are told about these rules before they begin playing. List some rules of a video game that you are familiar with:

_____

_____

In games like football and baseball, the **Code of Conduct** is stated in the rules for playing the game and typically the players are told about these rules before they begin playing.

List some rules for football, baseball or any other sport that you are familiar with:

_____

_____

In a marriage, the **Code of Conduct** often includes the rules of being trustworthy, respectful, and loving. List some of the rules that you believe your parents/guardians practice. If you don't know the rules your parents/guardians agree on, then ask them:

_____

_____

_____

All libraries have a **Code of Conduct.** What do you think the rules are?

_____

_____

_____

Write a **Code of Conduct** that you are familiar with. Think about what the **Code of Conduct** is for bowling, attending a dance, going to school, or within your family:

_____

_____

In both a friendship as well as a dating relationship, this **Code of Conduct** is created through many discussions and exchanges of ideas as you and your partner come to a mutual understanding and agreement as to what the rules should be.

This **Code of Conduct** will allow you and your friend or dating partner to improve your discussions as you agree on what to expect from each other and from the relationship. This process helps you build trust and work towards achieving your mutual goals. In most relationships, this code is unspoken and develops over time. In the most successful relationships, the **Code of Conduct** is discussed and agreed on by both partners as early in the relationship as possible.

In a **Healthy Relationship**, you and your partner will investigate and discuss your expectations of each other in the relationship. If your expectations match, then you can create and commit to living by the rules you agree to together.

When you ignore, violate or break the **Code of Conduct** rules in any setting, you may destroy trust, create pain, and may even break up the relationship. You may end up failing each other and yourself. When you discuss, agree, and commit to this shared **Code of Conduct**, you build trust and a solid relationship.

The Four Rules of any Successful Relationship

We have found that any successful relationship between two or more people is based upon four simple rules. Relationships and the people in them are disturbed and even damaged when these four rules are overlooked and not thought of as important. In the following subchapters we will explain these four rules, and the activities will help you determine what you would like the terms of each rule to be in your relationship with the other person.

The Code of Conduct for a Healthy Relationship begins with four simple rules that you can use to fit the needs of any relationship: parent to child, teacher to student, friendship, business relationship, and dating situation.

1. **Be trustworthy**
2. **Be respectful**
3. **Communicate openly, honestly, and directly**
4. **Work towards shared goals**

To build a **Healthy Relationship**, you must first think about each one of these four rules and ask yourself:
- What does it mean to me?
- How will I discuss the meaning with the other person?
- How will we develop and agree to our **Code of Conduct** under each of the four rules?

What does it mean to be trustworthy?

- ☐ Being reliable.
- ☐ Being honest.
- ☐ Friends who have each other's back.

How do you know when someone is trustworthy?

_____

_____

What does it mean to be respectful?

- ☐ First, it's being respectful to yourself by treating yourself well.
- ☐ Treating someone the way he/she wants to be treated.
- ☐ Thinking about the results of your behavior prior to your actions.

How can you tell if someone is being respectful?

_____

_____

What does it mean to communicate openly, honestly, and directly?

_____

_____

What does it mean to have shared goals?

☐ Together you discuss and agree about what it is that you want from the relationship.

☐ Together you discuss what your needs are.

☐ Together you communicate respectfully, and honestly.

Activity

Identify Four Rules

After dating for over a year successfully, Tayler began sharing with Alex her love for cooking. Together they joined a cooking class. They developed a working relationship in the kitchen as it often took their ability to work together doing different tasks to make good food: to have several hot and cold dishes prepared correctly and finished together for serving. They communicated honestly and knew each had different strengths and likes in the kitchen and in their relationship. They respected each other's feelings and trusted one another.

Soon they learned that they also had the same future plans: they wanted to find a job in a restaurant, find an apartment in which to live, and begin their life together. This couple is still happily together today, and they continue to work together toward their common goals.

List how the four simple rules were used to establish a **Healthy Relationship** for Tayler and Alex:

_____

_____

Write out your agreed Code of Conduct with the person with whom you have discussed the four rules.

Our agreed upon relationship's Code of Conduct is…

_____

_____

_____

Would you just walk into a clothing store and buy articles of clothing without trying them on first? Would you go into an electronics store and just buy any phone? Would you buy a car without first doing some research?

You know that having a relationship with any person needs the same investigative process. A **Healthy Relationship** is like standing in the middle of a bunch of rings or hula-hoops that fit inside each other, with the biggest one on the outside and the smallest one in the inside. Each ring represents a stage that must be processed before you move onto the next ring. When we meet someone we start out with the biggest and the outermost circle. As we get to know them and move through the different stages, we grow from being an acquaintance to becoming friends. We may eventually move from friends to becoming best friends. You may be emotionally intimate with your friends as well as your dating partner. We move from the bigger circles to smaller ones and become closer to each other as we move toward the inner circle.

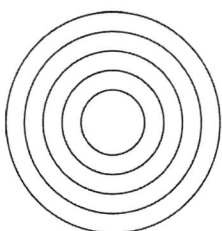

Our mascot the **SNAIL** and its shell is very useful here. The rings of the snail's shell are like the concentric circles above. They represent the different levels or **Stages of a Healthy Relationship**. If you skip or ignore one, you'll get into trouble when you get to the next stage. You need to make sure that you spend time investigating and communicating in a stage before moving to the next stage. This investigation is important in building **Healthy Relationships** that will last and be rewarding to both people.

Think about building with blocks. You begin with the first row, and if it is strong, you can add the second row. If the second row is stable then you can add the third. Once the third row is stable then you can add a fourth, fifth, and sixth. Each level of blocks needs to be carefully placed so that the next row can easily fit without knocking down the entire structure. A good foundation is needed for any **Healthy Relationship**.

Stages of Healthy Relationships

Please refer to our mascot below. As we have already shared, relationships are created over time as we investigate one another. Our process begins with Stage 1 on the outside of the snail's shell. This is where you begin to investigate and create a relationship. The information that we have presented in each stage is to be used as a guide as you get to know the person of interest. Notice that as you move from one stage to another you get closer to the inside of the snail's shell, or the smallest inner circle.

What happens as you get closer to the inner part of our snail? The space gets smaller. This growth from the outside towards the inside represents the relationships that we have over a lifetime. We have many more acquaintances than friends and many more friends than intimate relationships.

Stage 1 Meeting/social context: Checking each other out to see how similar or different you are socially. This is when you are acquaintances. You are investigating each other and your friendship.

Stage 2 Hanging out daily and figuring it out: Are we dating? Do we have a relationship? Begin to discuss and agree on the four rules: Shared Trust, Shared Respect, Effective Communication and Shared Goals.

Stage 3 Time together at school and community: Continue to create the **Code of Conduct**.

Stage 4 Testing the limits of the relationship: Balancing school, friends, family, & relationships privately and socially. This is usually when the disagreements and conflict begin.

Stage 6 Emotional/Physical intimacy: using the five principles of decision making to pick the right person, the right time and place.

Stage 5 Emotional intimacy: Trusting each other to get close & sharing feelings and sensitivities. Realizing that the relationship can handle conflict and moving towards the 6th stage.

It is important to realize that these stages are connected and interrelated. Each stage has multiple layers. Couples go through these stages over and over again adding depth to their relationship.

Stage 1

Meeting/ Social context

This is when you first meet or become aware of each other. You have just a slight knowledge of one another. People in this stage are typically acquaintances. Maybe the person is familiar because you have both attended the same events, community group, bowling group, or class. Maybe you have already said "Hello" to one another. Or maybe you have met and are completely head-over-heels at the first glance.

This is the stage where you are checking each other out and gathering information to see how similar or different you are. You will decide if what you're feeling is a crush or something deeper and decide to approach each other during this stage.

Stage 2

Hanging out daily: figuring it out.

This is the stage where you have spoken and are hanging out daily together, but with other friends around. Eventually, you are more comfortable with it being just the two of you.

You may even consider these questions:

- Do we have a relationship?
- Should we date each other?
- What will the relationship be like?

In stage 2, you begin to set and match your expectations and develop and set the **Code of Conduct** for how you will interact and relate to each other.

Stage 3

Time together at school and community (dances/bowling alley/movies/social functions and other functions together).

As we mentioned before, any successful relationship between two or more people is based upon four simple rules of shared **Trust**, shared **Respect**, effective **Communication** and shared **Goals**. During this stage, as you interact with each other privately and with others, you will begin to learn how you each can trust, respect, and communicate and determine if, as a couple, you have shared goals and intentions. You and your dating partner will also begin to create an agreed upon **Code of Conduct**.
In most relationships, especially early on, each person may assume that the other person shares the same values and code, only to find out later that they don't. So communication is the key. Don't assume – instead, discuss and talk about what you want the rules of your relationship to be. Make sure that you include and honor our four rules, because when these rules are overlooked and/or broken, couples and relationships suffer.

Stage 4

Testing the limits of the relationship.

During this stage, the couple is usually trying to balance school/work, friends, family and the relationship privately and socially. You may have your first misunderstanding, fight, or even break up here as you test the limits (or what the relationship can tolerate) and challenge the **Code of Conduct**. You will also face miscommunications and disappointments. You will also have to learn how to be forgiven and apologize when you hurt each other. We will talk about this more in the next chapter on Effective Communication.

Stage 5

Emotional intimacy.

As you go through the above stages, you will create emotional lessons that you teach and learn from each other. This is when you spend as much time as you can with each other and trust each other with your secrets, fears, worries, hopes and wishes. You protect each other and function as a couple. Couples will also seek each other's opinion and consider the other person's feelings and preferences when making decisions.

The Think-Twice Step: Step 6

The step of Serious Adult Consequences: Physical Intimacy.

This is when you have earned each other's respect, trust and have discussed and agreed on your goals for your relationship. You have talked about sex openly, honestly and you both are able and willing to handle the consequences of having sex. The decision to do so is something that you both want and it doesn't violate any of our **Five Principles of Healthy Decision Making** (discussed later in the workbook). Remember, sex is an adult act with adult consequences and you both must be able and willing to deal with these consequences if you want to engage each other sexually. More importantly, having sex does not make you an adult.

Snail Wisdom

It is very important to understand that the physical aspect of a Healthy Relationship is a process that should develop over time. So many people get into this stage before completing the others. This is a sure way to create confusion, drama, and pain.

Remember that a relationship is a living thing that is in a constant state of growth and development. It must be looked after and cared for by both people, individually and together. Ultimately, when couples complete, share, and process each stage successfully, they create a relationship that enhances them individually and promotes their well being in all aspects of their individual and shared life. The more a couple works on their relationship, the deeper and more meaningful these stages become.

A **Healthy Relationship** is also a learning and teaching process where two people who are attracted to each other spend time to teach and learn how they each view life and the world. Together and through this investigation, they will figure out if they are well matched and agree to commit to each other.

Activity
Match the scenario with one of the six stages

Stage 1 Meeting in social/context _____

Stage 2 Hanging out daily: figuring it out _____

Stage 3 Time together at school and community _____

Stage 4 Testing the limits of the relationship _____

Stage 5 Emotional intimacy _____

Stage 6 Physical intimacy & sex _____

Scenarios: Place the letter by the corresponding stage.

a. Lee and Blake have known each other for a couple of months and have begun to think about whether they should date. They are beginning to discuss and agree on the four rules of their relationship.

b. Laurie and Brian are in their late twenties and have been dating successfully for over two years. They have negotiated conflicts and have an open and honest communication system that works. They trust each other and are not afraid to share their true feelings.

c. Alex and Sam are taking an adult education class together and have just exchanged email addresses.

d. Drew and Catherine have been investigating their relationship at school and in the community. Together they are building their **Code of Conduct**.

e. Kyle and Natasha have been together for a while privately and socially. They are finding that they don't always agree on where to go and what to do. Sometimes they even find that they disagree with how they treat one another.

f. Linda and Jack have been dating for five years and are in love. They get along very well and all of their friends recognize that they belong together. They are engaged to be married.

Let's review...

A **Healthy Relationship** between any two people, regardless of friendship or dating relationship needs to be built on shared trust, respect, effective communication, and common goals.

Each person must be okay with occasionally being wrong, be open to hearing about it and be willing to learn from the other and make the necessary changes to improve the relationship.

Basically, relationships are like a dance where each person works to help the other person dance better. It involves practice and learning how to dance without stepping on each other's toes.

Think of three couples you may know who have **Healthy Relationships**. List why you think their relationships are healthy:

_____

_____

What are the important qualities of a **Healthy Relationship**?

_____

_____

Shared Trust

Trust is probably the most important aspect of any relationship between two or more people. You build trust as you experience the other as someone who is sincere, safe, reliable, and has your back. Trust develops over time when you say what you mean and mean what you say. **Shared Trust** happens when the actions and words of two people match their thoughts and feelings, and when they follow through on the things to which they commit. When there's an alignment between what you think, feel, say, and do, others will experience you as **sincere** and **authentic**. This is a quality that people are wired to sense and detect in each other as they interact (get to know one another). When we sense sincerity, we trust.

People naturally and continuously scan (look at) others for any threats that they may pose and for how safe they are. Unfortunately, at times, people choose to ignore the results of their scans and move forward. They believe that they can change what they sense about the other person.

Some people become experts at fooling others. These people are the most dangerous. They can cover up the most insincere intentions (behaviors/motives) and hurt you. This is why developing trust must take time. When building friendships and dating relationships you must experience each other in different settings and over time, to ensure your safety both emotionally and physically.

> **Snail Trail…**
>
> Kayla and David have been going out for three weeks. Kayla went over to David's house around 4:00 pm to study for a test and to go out for burgers with his family at 6:00 pm. She forgot to leave her parents a note and left her cell phone behind. When she got to David's, his parents were not home. David said that they left to run some errands. Around 5:00 pm, Kayla, who had not had lunch and was hungry, noticed a big, unopened bag of candy and asked David if she could have some to hold her over until dinner. He became somewhat upset and said that he didn't want to share the candy.
>
> David did not offer Kayla anything else to eat. Kayla was disappointed but didn't say anything. David asked her if she wanted to go for a swim in his pool.

 **Snail Talk**

First of all, Kayla should have left a note or sent a text before leaving home, letting her parents/guardians know where she was going. You should always tell the person who is responsible for you where you are going. In addition, knowing someone for only two to three weeks is not enough time to build a trusting relationship. When Kayla arrived at David's home and his parents weren't in, Kayla should have asked about where they were and when they'd be back.

Next, David's unwillingness to share his candies with someone he likes and, more importantly, not offering to take care of Kayla's need (she was hungry), is a warning sign. David will probably be controlling, selfish, and not very compassionate in his relationship with Kayla.

Lastly, no one was home and David now wants Kayla to get into a bathing suit and get into the water. If she does, she will be placing herself in a very vulnerable position and anything could happen.

Snail Wisdom

When you trust someone, you are not afraid to give your all and to open your heart. It's like "going belly up". This is what your dogs or cats do at some point every day, at some point, when they lie on their backs and take a little nap. They know that they are safe and that no one is going to attack them in the most vulnerable part of their body, their belly.

Snail Talk

Sharing trust in a relationship keeps you secure and creates the feeling of belonging. It allows friends/couples to share secrets, feelings, and needs without feeling selfish or self-conscience. Together they believe that the information shared will be kept a secret and not used to harm them at a later point even if there is an argument or a break up.

What can you do to earn someone's trust?

- [ ] Keep his/her secrets.
- [ ] Do what you say you will do.
- [ ] Keep his/her safety in mind.

How do you know that someone trusts you?

_____

_____

How do you know that you really trust someone?

_____

_____

Many people trust others in different ways and with different amounts of information. You may share secrets with your family that you don't share with your friends or vice-versa and that is okay. Many people find it difficult to really trust someone with one hundred percent of themselves. However, it is important to trust people so that you can form relationships. So, trust as much as you are comfortable doing and realize that people will let you down from time to time, but you will often come out of relationships much stronger than when you had started.

Snail Wisdom

It is possible to love someone and not trust them. For example, you may love your neighbor and not trust him/her. You can trust someone and not emotionally love them. For example, you can trust your teacher or your doctor and you may not love them.

Snail Talk

Maurice and Kristin had only been dating four months when she felt that she trusted him so much she could share some of her deepest secrets with him, things that no one else knew. Maurice felt the same way and shared his secrets with her knowing that it would be safe and they could discuss their feelings openly and honestly.

List three people that you trust and tell the reasons why:

1.

2.

3.

List three reasons why others should see you as trustworthy:

1.

2.

3.

You can earn trust by not abusing a person's trust in you and by keeping his/her secrets. You always keep his/her best interests in mind and try not to hurt him/her on purpose. You prove yourself over time with your honesty and respect for his/her values, needs and sensitivities. Trust takes time to build and yet it can be lost so easily.

Snail Wisdom

Trust is so easy to break but really hard to regain. Once someone breaks your trust it can take a really long time to rebuild.

> Snail Trails…
>
> Ling had his heart broken when he found out that Jessie had been sending romantic texts to two other guys and changed her relationship status to single. He got many messages from his friends asking him about his relationship with Jessie.
>
> This was the second time that Jessie had broken his trust, and he was done. He decided that he wasn't going to trust Jessie ever again.

Explain a time when someone broke your trust:

_____

_____

If your trust was broken, explain what you did. If you haven't experienced a time when your trust was broken, explain how you think you might handle having your trust broken:

_____

_____

Trust that is broken can be rebuilt. A person must work hard at regaining trust with their words, actions, and promises.

Snail talk

People who experience broken trust often take and continue their pain, injury, and distrust into future relationships. This is where our mascot the **SNAIL** comes in handy again. Remember that **SNAIL**s create and leave a trail behind. This trail becomes our history and it is our past experiences that we carry into our relationships. You may have heard some people refer to this as "having baggage."

Think back on any relationships that have hurt you. What are the feelings you still remember?

_____

_____

What are some of the things that you can do to make sure that you don't break a friend's trust?

☐ Always have the person's best interests in mind.

☐ Keep his/her secrets unless he/she is in danger.

☐ If I say I will do something, I will do it.

Write a summary about the importance of **Shared Trust**:

_____
_____
_____

Shared Respect

Respect is considering someone else's rights, values, boundaries, feelings and sensitivities as you interact with him/her. Another rule of a **Healthy Relationship** is **Shared Respect**. **Shared Respect** is agreeing to consider each other's wants and needs as we interact with each other and the world around us. It is the ability to tell someone that you are not happy with his/her behavior and to be able to do so without attacking or damaging his/her self-esteem or the relationship. It is the willingness to consider the impact your behavior and words may have on the other person and your relationship with him/her. It includes the willingness to apologize, ask for forgiveness, and to forgive.

> ### Let's review…
>
> Respect is the willingness to ask yourself: "How will my actions, words and decisions impact the other person or our relationship?" Or, considering: "How can I tell my friend/date/the other that I don't like something that he/she said or did without hurting him/her or making him/her feel badly?
>
> Friends and couples that mutually respect each other keep these questions in mind as they interact with each other. Their common purpose is to enhance their relationship by respecting each other's wishes, values, boundaries, and sensitivities. The goal is to "make each other's day" while having fun.

 Snail Wisdom

When you interact with people in general, you show respect by knocking on the door before entering a room, or by holding the door open for another, or by asking if a seat is taken before sitting, or by giving your seat up for an elderly person.

You show respect by being polite and saying things like "Please" and "Thank You." List some occasions when you commonly show respect:

_____

_____

List some occasions when you don't show respect but should:

_____

_____

You also show respect by not making people feel uncomfortable for being different. For example, maybe the way they're dressed is odd and different from the way you dress. Instead, you should try to keep those thoughts to yourself. You should follow the same rule when you think that someone's preference for a food item or activity is odd and different from what you like.

Think of a time when someone has commented on something that you liked because they thought it was unusual or odd. How did it make you feel?

_____

_____

Think of a time when you made a comment about something that someone has liked because you thought it was unusual or odd. How do you think you made the person feel?

_____

_____

When you first meet someone, you put your best foot forward. This means that you go above and beyond what you do normally to create a positive impression. However, as you become comfortable in a relationship, you may stop considering how your actions will affect the other and tend to view your relationship as successful if you are able to say and do as you please. Be mindful that this attitude is risky, and you may be hurting your relationship.

A successful relationship is one in which each person works hard to be the best that he/she can be and this means considering the impact that your words, actions, and decisions will have on the other person before moving ahead.

> **Snail Trail...**
>
> Greg and Jill had been dating for about a month when he noticed that Jill was really not patient with her siblings and parents. In front of Greg, Jill had lied to her parents. She said that they were on their way to the movies when instead they had plans to hang out at the beach with friends. Jill lost her temper easily with her siblings and had a tough time seeing the part she played. She always blamed others.

Snail Talk

Shared Respect in a **Healthy Relationship** means that the couple interacts and behaves while considering the impact of their words, actions, and decisions on each other.

Jill's impatient attitude with her siblings and parents could easily carry over into her relationship with Greg.

Additionally, her lie about where she and Greg would be going shows that she lacks respect for herself and her parents, again indicating that in the near future she is likely to lie to Greg.

Remember Pink Flags

Pink Flags are small but important signals that people and couples experience with each other and may choose to ignore. These events and experiences, if ignored, may eventually lead to **Red Flags** and, if ignored, create disappointment and pain.

Snail Wisdom

The first step to respecting others is to respect yourself.

List some of the ways that you can respect yourself:

- ☐ Do what I say that I am going to do.
- ☐ Make sure that my friends know how I like to be treated and what I don't like.
- ☐ Make sure that I am dressed neatly and that I am clean.

List some ways that you can demonstrate respect towards your friend/date:

_____

_____

List some of the ways that the adults in your life show respect towards each other while disagreeing:

- [ ] They don't scream at one another.
- [ ] They listen to what one another is saying.
- [ ] They agree to disagree and walk away friends.

Let's review…

Shared respect means that you respect the stages for developing a **Healthy Relationship** and work your way through them one by one. See SNAIL diagram page 81.

First, you meet the other, in person or online.

Next, you decide to approach him/her or are approached by him/her. Always keep your safety in mind.

Eventually you agree to meet for that first date, and the investigation process begins.

Tell your parent/guardian/friend where you are going and arrange for your parent/guardian/friend to call you at different times during the date. Better yet, bring your parent/guardian/friend along on the first several dates.

It is important to realize that respect for oneself or other means that you do not become demanding or aggressive, physically or sexually. End the relationship/date if for any reason you feel unsafe or uncomfortable.

Snail Wisdom

Relationships take time, and one key component to any Healthy Relationship is respecting each other.

Effective Communication

The most important aspect of any relationship is **communication.** It is **IMPOSSIBLE NOT TO COMMUNICATE**. You are always communicating, even when you sleep; you are always in the process of giving and getting information to and from your surroundings. So even when sleeping, you will adjust your blankets as you get cold or warm. Even when you are out cold on an operating table, your blood pressure and heartbeat tells the doctor how to adjust your medications.

When it comes to communication, research has shown that your words are only a small part of what you are communicating. Your voice or how you say things is a bigger part, and the biggest part is your body language. Your body language is what you do with your body as you speak. Body language includes your body movements, gestures, and facial expressions as you speak. This is why sometimes when a store clerk tells you to "have a nice day," you know that they don't mean it, because their tone of voice or body language were different from their words.

In any relationship we communicate how we feel and what we think not just with our words, but also with our voice and body language. When our words, our voice, and our actions match, the listener experiences us as sincere. You communicate your feelings and thoughts to your friend or date, not just with your words and voice, but also with your actions.

Activity
Everyone communicates

What are you communicating when you are smiling?

_____

_____

What are you communicating when you look someone in the eyes while they are speaking with you?

_____

_____

What are you communicating when you have an angry face?

_____

_____

What are you communicating when you're not looking at the person speaking with you?

_____

_____

What are you communicating when your arms are folded across your chest and you're leaning back while someone is speaking to you?

_____

_____

What are you communicating when your voice is loud and you are speaking rapidly?

_____

_____

What are you communicating when you storm out of a room?

_____

_____

What are you communicating when you're texting while someone is speaking to you?

_____

_____

A **Healthy Relationship** involves communication. For the communication to be effective, each party must listen and speak from the heart. This means being honest with yourself and with your friend or date. It means that you talk about what is in your heart even when it makes you feel uncomfortable, awkward, or anxious. It also means that you talk about what is in your heart even if you believe that it may make the other person feel uncomfortable or awkward.

Snail Wisdom

Always look for alignment. Ask yourself: Does the other person's behavior match what they are saying to me?

As we mentioned above, have you ever gone to a store and, when you left, the salesperson told you to have a nice day and you knew that they didn't mean it? How did you know? Your ears helped you figure out if the salesperson said the right words. The salesperson did, but there was something in his/her voice that didn't sound very friendly; he/she sounded bored or not interested. You watched his/her actions and you noticed that he/she didn't even lift his/her head to look at you as he/she told you to have a nice day.

Your heart will be checking people for sincerity as you listen and look. In this case, you experience the salesperson as not sincere as you leave. Sincere people are people whose thoughts, feelings, and actions match.

This is also true in all relationships, especially a **Healthy Relationship**. If your eyes, ears, and heart all tell you that the other person means what they say, then you can trust them and move forward.

Snail Wisdom

Effective communication is like a window with each person accepting the responsibility to keep his/her side of the glass clean so that each person can see and hear one another.

Think of the people that you enjoy communicating with the most and list why:

_____

_____

Think of the people that you believe enjoy communicating with you and list why:

_____

_____

How can you change your communications so that others want to hear what it is that you have to say?

- [ ] Listen well.
- [ ] Don't make judgments.
- [ ] Be respectful and honest.
- [ ] Encourage the other person to speak.

What role does your body language play in communication?

_____

_____

What role does the pitch of your voice play in communication?

___

> **Let's review...**
>
> Effective communication does **NOT** occur without active listening. Active listening means that you must temporarily prevent making a judgment and instead listen for feelings and meanings to truly understand what your partner is saying. It is the willingness to listen, hear, and understand what the other person is saying before trying to get them to listen, hear, and understand you.
>
> Together you agree to talk about your likes and dislikes, your hopes and fears, and what irks and angers you. You also share what pleases and delights you.
>
> The goal is not to be right, or to change the other, but to increase mutual understanding and work towards your **Shared Goals**.

Activity

Honest communication

How did the girls work out their conflict of both liking Jon?

___

Most people are comfortable with communicating when things are going well and there are no disagreements. However, most of us are uncomfortable when disagreements arise and there is a conflict. Resolving conflict is an important part of communicating effectively.

Conflict is a natural and normal part of any relationship between two or more people. Conflict usually occurs when people disagree, experience a great deal of emotion about what they each perceive, want to prove their point, and want to be right or win the argument. Conflict can also happen when one person feels wronged by another. Usually when this happens, people react by either withdrawing or becoming visibly upset. This may result in a fight and the argument may resolve when one or both people acknowledge the impact of their words or actions on another person and apologize.

We have all learned the importance of apologizing when we realize that we have done something wrong, but not everyone knows how to apologize effectively. Another factor that most people overlook is that just because someone apologizes, it does not mean that they are forgiven. Without apologizing and forgiving appropriately, relationships will eventually become unhealthy and in many instances end. So, to build and maintain healthy relationships, we must learn to acknowledge our mistakes and apologize, take responsibility to fix things, make changes, and ask to be forgiven.

Let's review…

When you disagree with someone, you must…
- Set up a time to discuss your concerns privately
- Try to understand the other's side before trying to be understood
- Focus on the behavior
- Support the other person
- Be specific
- Use "I" statements (Practice with "I" statements on pg 94)
- Listen

When you disagree with someone, do not…
- Discuss your concerns publicly
- Defend your position before knowing the whole story
- Don't attack the person or their self esteem
- Don't make general statements
- Avoid using the terms "always" and "never"
- Don't use "You" statements

Good apologies have seven steps:

1. Begin with admitting that you are very sorry for causing pain.

2. Ask for and listen to the other person tell his/her story.

3. Acknowledge that it shouldn't have happened and validate the other person's feelings.

4. Next ask, "What can I do or say to be forgiven?"

5. If he/she is willing to forgive, discuss what needs to be done.

6. Change your behavior.

7. The last step is to ask for forgiveness.

Practice writing an appropriate apology by using the above seven steps:

_____

_____

_____

Snail Wisdom

The manner in which your parents/adults in your life disagreed with each other and resolved conflict as you were growing up becomes your pattern for how to address and resolve conflict in relationships. You can learn from their mistakes and improve your approach.

Do you think that people who love each other should disagree?

_____

_____

How should you disagree with a loved one?

_____

_____

Recall a time when someone disagreed with you. How did it make you feel?

_____

_____

If someone were to disagree with you what would you like them to say and do?

- ☐ Explain his/her point of view respectfully.
- ☐ Agree to disagree and maintain our friendship.
- ☐ Be polite and respect my feelings.

How would you tell someone that you disagree with them without hurting his/her feelings?

_____

_____

Taking responsibility for your feelings is a very important aspect of good communication skills. One of the best ways to do this is to use "I" statements. These are sentences that begin with I.

"**I feel** _____ (fill in the blank) **when you** _____ (fill in the blank)

because _____ (fill in the blank) **and what I want is** _____ (fill in the blank)."

Activity

Let's practice some "I" statements

Your best friend says that you will get together on the weekend. The weekend comes and goes and your best friend doesn't call. Write an "I" message that describes how you might feel:

_____

_____

Your best friend appears to be flirting with your date. You want him/her to stop. Write an "I" message that describes how you might feel:

_____

_____

Imagine someone not following through with a commitment. Write an "I" message that describes how you might feel:

_____

_____

As we have mentioned before, conflict can happen in any relationship. It is important that you address the conflict openly, honestly, and respectfully. When conflict can't be resolved or a person is unwilling to take responsibility for their part in the conflict and continues to engage in behaviors that adversely affect you, it may be time to end the relationship. You must recognize **Pink** and **Red Flags** because they are signs that we must distance ourselves from the person.

Shared Goals

Creating a **Healthy Relationship** is like creating a garden in your back yard with another person. Your garden will not look nor function well if you would like roses and your partner would like a sand and cactus theme. The garden will look best if you both agree on what you want it to look like and share the daily efforts of caring for the garden. In your garden you must keep the insects and weeds under control just like in your relationship you must keep it free of things that destroy its beauty and purpose. To create a garden that you both enjoy requires both people to discuss, agree, and share their goals. This is why developing **Shared Goals** is an important aspect of developing a **Healthy Relationship**.

Creating **Shared Goals** is about your willingness and desire to communicate your needs, wants, fears, worries, and concerns openly, honestly, and respectfully. This is needed in order for you to decide what you want for yourself and from your relationship.

Together, you and your friend/boyfriend/girlfriend build a relationship that is not only enjoyable to you, but also brings joy to others as they see you get along well and care for each other and the relationship.

Snail Wisdom

Shared Goals are what allow people to create and maintain so many different relationships. Having Shared Goals holds friendships together.

What are your current goals?

_____

_____

What goals do you have in common with your family?

_____

_____

What goals do you have in common with your friends?

_____

_____

What are your future goals?

_____

_____

What will you need in order to achieve your goals?

_____

_____

What will you need in order to develop the same goals with another person?

_____

_____

Let's review...

Creating **Shared Goals** is working with another person who has the same intentions as you do. To do this right, you must communicate effectively. Effective communication is all about respectful, open, and honest discussions, and most importantly, it's about listening. Discussing and agreeing on your **Shared Goals** will help your relationship be what you both want.

Creating **Shared Goals** involves making decisions personally and with other people. Most of our lives are based on decisions that we or others make. Making **Healthy Decisions** can be complicated or confusing, especially when we want to be liked and are in the process of getting to know someone. There are many things that influence our decision-making process. Things like peer pressure, the desire to fit in, and our values and morals are very powerful. They impact our decision-making process.

We have discovered that if people apply our **Five Principles of Healthy Decision Making** before they make their choices, they will end up with good decisions and good results. Next time you tune into the news on your smart phone, TV, or radio, pay attention to all the people who made poor choices and now face the consequences of their decisions. Chances are that they have violated one or more of our principles; otherwise, they would not be in trouble. These principles apply to all aspects of life. To make the best decisions consider the questions under each principle as you go about making a decision. <u>***A healthy decision does not violate any of the 5 principles.***</u>

The Five Principles of Healthy Decision Making:

1. **It must be Legal. Ask:** Is the decision and its consequences legal? Would you get into trouble with the law?

2. **It must be Ethical. Ask:** Is the decision and its consequences morally right or wrong? If your choice was disclosed to others would it embarrass you or your family?

3. **It must be Safe at all levels. Ask:** Is the decision and its consequences safe? Consider different forms of safety.

    a) Physiologically safety (body). Ask: How will it affect my/our/another's physical health and well being?

    b) Psychologically safety (mind). Ask: How will it affect my/our/another's psychological/emotional well being?

    c) Socially safety. Ask: How will it affect my/our/other's social situations and social well being?

4. **It must be Appropriate. Ask:** Given my role(s) and responsibilities, if someone took a photo of me/us doing what I/we have decided to do: "Will I/we be okay and proud to have it appear on the nightly news?" or "Will I/we be embarrassed and want to leave town?"

5. **It must be aligned with your Value system. Ask:** Is the decision and its consequences in alignment with my/your/our personal and familial values? Would you tell your parents?

Think about a poor decision that you have made or have seen or heard of and list below which of our 5 principles it violated:

_____

_____

_____

Activity

Match the principle and the scenario. Place the letter next to the number

1. Legal_____

2. Ethical_____

3. Safety_____

4. Appropriate given the person's role_____

5. Value system_____

   a. Jerry is 25 and Sandy is 17; they have started having sex. What principle are they violating? Place the letter by the number.

   b. Maria really wants to have sex with her boyfriend Bob. Bob is unsure if he is ready for an intimate relationship. Maria forces herself on Bob. What principle are they violating?

   c. Janet is 20 years old. One night Michael, Janet's friend, was out to dinner with his parents and saw Janet smoking a cigarette. Michael's mom said, "Isn't that Janet?" What principle is she violating?

   d. Alex and Sam meet at church in the parking lot and leave shortly after their arrival and go to breakfast. Their parents believe that they are at church. What principle are they violating?

   e. Tom was on a first date and Sam insisted on driving faster than the speed limit so that they wouldn't be late to the movies. What principle are they violating?

Snail Wisdom

Being the right person is just as important as finding the right person.

What can you do to be the right person?

- [ ] Be respectful.
- [ ] Be honest.
- [ ] Be trustworthy.

Becoming Friends

Moving from an acquaintance to a friendship happens over time as you get to know one another and develop shared **Trust**, **Respect** and common **Goals**. It takes effort and **Effective Communication** to build a friendship. Remember that building a friendship takes time, and you need to move slowly and safely.

After you meet someone who you think you would like to develop a relationship with there are several signs that you may look for to tell if they are also interested in you.

Let's review…

You know that someone is interested in being your friend when he/she behave in the following ways:

- Your friend talks with you. You don't have to talk everyday or all the time. Your friend shares what he/she is thinking and what's going on in his/her life that is important. Your friend wants to know the same information about you.

- Your friend smiles at you and compliments you.

- A friend knows your phone number and how to get in touch with you.

- A friend says things that make you laugh and you feel good when you are around him/her.

- You do things together: play video games, attend activities, share meals, and exchange gifts.

- A friend understands your challenges and is willing to be there for you when you are sad, mad, and not feeling well.

- A friend invites you over to his/her home and shares things with you.

- You know each other's family members, pets, and favorite foods, favorite television shows, favorite movies, favorite musical artist, and favorite activities.

- A friend asks for forgiveness and is willing to forgive you.

What personal things do you like to share with a friend?

What types of personal things do you like that friends share with you?

What compliments do you like to hear about yourself?

What are your favorite activities?

What are you afraid of?

What types of things make you upset?

 Snail Wisdom

Only you can determine if you are ready for friendship or dating. Always remember that your safety and comfort comes first. Only engage in behaviors that do NOT cause you or the other person harm, embarrassment, or regret, now or later.

Understanding friends and friendships

When Friends share the following:	You can expect:
Phone numbers	They would like to be called
Social Media contact information	They would like to be in touch using the internet
Interests, likes and dislikes	To learn about your interests, likes and dislikes
The desire to hang out with you	They enjoy your company
Feelings and sensitivities	They want you to respect and be sensitive to their needs
Secrets	They want you to keep it to yourself
Background and story	Want you to know who they are
Their resources	They expect you to be generous with yours
Their home and their family	They expect you to understand them even more

What can you do to be a good friend?

_____

_____

_____

It is always important to think about your friend and try to make him/her happy. You can make him/her happy by providing him/her with things you know he/she likes and in return they do the same for you. This could be as simple as getting each other a beverage or just sharing a good laugh.

Think about one of your friends; what could you do that they would appreciate?

_____

_____

Activity

Friendship

Jan didn't have to get Kate a coffee. Doing so makes Kate feel thought of and valued. Friends think of one another and anticipate each other's needs even when they may not be in the same place at the same time. Bringing your friends gifts or sending texts tells them that you are thinking of them and that you value the relationship.

Chapter 7

Sweet Emotions

Crush vs Love

Sweet Emotions

Once you have met and spent some time moving through the **Stages of a Healthy Relationship** (see page 75) you may begin to experience strong feelings towards the other person. Some people feel confused about the intensity (strength) of their emotions and are not sure if they are in love or whether they have just a crush. There is a difference between having a crush and being in love with someone.

One of the definitions of love is an intense feeling of deep passion. Love isn't just something you say to someone because they asked you to be their significant other. LOVE is an action word. Once you say it, you are saying: "I do and will love you with my **words, thoughts, actions**, and **decisions**." You are saying that you will regard the person that you love as special and that you will cherish them. It means that you like him/her enough to share your time, your things, and your life with him/her freely.

A crush can be defined as experiencing strong emotions towards someone that you really don't know.

Listed below are some of the differences between having a crush and being in love.

A crush can:

- Be a strong attraction to someone that you don't really know.
- Be unrealistic, long-or short-lasting and can happen at any time.
- Make you ignore your loved one's faults and flaws. A crush can mislead you into thinking that you are in love.
- Make your imagination get the best of you. A crush can make you blind to reality. Your crush may actually be in a relationship with someone else and you won't believe it.
- Make you think that you have a relationship with someone, even though you may never have.

True love:

- Takes time, hard work, and commitment.
- Makes you see and accept your loved one's faults and flaws.
- Makes you feel like your life has color and that your loved one can do no wrong.
- Makes you want to know all that you can about the other person.
- Brings out the best in you and in the other person.
- Makes you think about the future with that person.

It is natural for friends to feel love and strong emotions toward each other. It's okay to tell someone who is of the same sex and is a friend that you love him/her. Sometimes two people become close without being sexually attracted to one another. Instead they share an admiration and love for each other and what they each bring to the relationship. As previously described, a **Healthy Relationship** can make you become better than you were before knowing the other person.

> Snail Trails…
>
> Tom shares that he thinks his sister's friend Rosie is very cute. Even though he doesn't know her, he has a giant crush on her. He convinces his sister to set him up on a date with Rosie.

Snail Talk

Not all crushes work out. Tom will have to investigate and move slowly.

> Snail Trails…
>
> Sonya and Adrian have been dating for three months. They are very happy with each other and there are still things that Adrian does not know about Sonya. Adrian shared, "I really like you." This made Sonya feel relieved and comfortable. Sometimes saying "I love you" too soon can make someone feel uncomfortable. They may feel that they have to live up to some things that they may not be ready for.

Snail Talk

Adrian shared his feelings appropriately. Just because you are with someone, you don't need to feel pressure to tell them that you love them. Love takes time to build. Adrian continues to build a **Healthy Relationship** by slowing down and taking time with Sonya to really get to know her.

Activity

I like you

Sometimes it is best not to jump right in and say, "I love you." Remember that relationships are built over time. You want to be sure that you really know the person and you do that by having different experiences in different settings with that person.

Who do you like?

_____

_____

Who do you love?

_____

_____

It is best to let your feelings of love develop over time. Pay attention to your feelings. If your feelings change, look for the reasons. Sometimes while people are investigating relationships their feelings change. Don't be quick to say, "I love you" too soon. If you do and then later you decide that you may want to just be friends, it may be too hard to go back to a friendship.

> **Snail Trail…**
>
> Lyn and Jed were having some troubles and Lyn kept reminding Jed that she loved him. Jed didn't feel loved and instead he felt confused. Without warning Lyn broke up with Jed.

 Snail Talk

Jed was very upset and couldn't understand how Lyn kept saying that she loved him and then broke up so suddenly. Consequently, Jed wanted nothing to do with Lyn. He didn't even want to be friends.

It is always important to let love grow. Remember, building **Healthy Relationships** takes place over time. Unfortunately, Lyn was too impatient and Jed just didn't feel the same way that she did. This may happen in a relationship. One person may be ready for the next steps while the other person may not.

 Snail Wisdom

When breaking up with someone it is best to end your relationship in a way that does not hurt how the other person feels about themselves.

> **Snail Trail…**
>
> Gail and Brody had only been dating a week when Brody started to act lovingly. He told Gail that he loved her. After about two weeks, Brody discovered that he really didn't love Gail and it was too hard to go back to just friends.

 Snail Talk

If you say, "I love you" before you really know it, you will have a hard time going back to just a friendship. Usually, when people say, "I love you" before they are sure, they might actually start to talk and act in unloving ways. They do this so the other person will get the message and decide to break up. This way, they won't have to be the bad one who ends the relationship.

If you start your relationship with saying, "I love you" it will be difficult to grow. You'll be stuck in your "I love you" stage with nowhere to go unless you have the intention of marrying them after less than 24 hours of dating (which doesn't happen very often)!

You shouldn't say you love someone unless you truly mean it. You don't want to go back on your word, or else you'll hurt your relationship and your future growth with the person.

Crush vs. Love

 Thoughts from our friends…

Lucy feels a crush is when you just really like someone.

Kevin says, "A crush is when you think about someone a lot and imagine yourself being with them."

Thomas shares, "When you have a crush on someone, the person may not feel the same way about you."

Catherine shares, "A crush is liking someone who turns out differently than you thought after time."

Kim shares, "I have crushes on movie stars."

Tony believes, "Crushes never last."

Sara says, "Crushes are a way of exploring an unknown."

Bill says, "A crush fizzles after time, and the person is no longer attractive."

Margie shared, "I will always keep my crush closed in my brain."

Tobin feels, "Crushes are worthwhile, they help you appreciate true love."

Have you ever had a crush? Describe what the crush felt like?

_____

_____

 Thoughts from our friends…

Jeanna shares, "Love is butterflies in the stomach, sweaty hands, heart pounding fast, can't control what you're saying while talking too fast, and blushing nervously with hot flashes."

Peter says, "When you love someone, the feelings are mutual."

Victor shares, "Love is serious and lasts for a long time."

Lucy shares, "I'm waiting to grow up to fall in love."

Aretha shares, "Being in love is like walking on a cloud every day as the magic continues to happen."

Thomas says, "Love is the best when it is mutual."

Frank shared, "I dream about meeting the right person some day and being in love."

Samantha says, "Love means never brushing your teeth alone."

Have you ever been in love? Describe how that felt?

_____

_____

_____

List the differences between having a crush and being in love:

_____

_____

Snail Wisdom

Relationships help us grow and when they end, the growth can be a part of us to take to other relationships.

Snail Talk

When dating, girls usually listen to determine how their partner feels about them and the relationship. If the guy says, "You're pretty and I love you," most girls feel attractive and loved. However, talk isn't enough. Always judge the person you are interested in by what they do as well as what they say.

Most boys react to how a girl looks and dresses. Some may measure how they feel about a girl by how they react to her appearance. The way the girl looks and dresses shouldn't be used as the only measure to decide if the person is right for you.

Snail Wisdom

Always compare what your date is saying against what your date is doing in all relationships and not just in the relationship they have with you.

> Snail Trail...
>
> Juan really likes Alicia, and they have been dating for about two months. Alicia spends a lot of time with other boys at dances and bowling. This makes Juan jealous.

Snail Talk

Juan needs to talk honestly with Alicia about how he feels about her behavior with other boys. He needs to find out if Alicia is really interested in him. He also needs to be prepared for Alicia to admit that she would rather be with other boys at this time. This can be very tricky, because the truth can hurt and no one likes feeling hurt. Therefore, sometimes to avoid being hurt, we choose to ignore the behaviors we see and only listen to what we are told.

Snail Wisdom

It is okay for our friends or someone that you are dating to be busy with other friends and other activities. Allowing your special someone to socialize and have their own independence is very important for the health of your relationship. Remember, your relationship is built on Effective Communication, Shared Trust, Respect, and Goals. By following these four rules partners can maintain their independence.

What are your thoughts?

_____

_____

How do you know when you are ready to move from friendship into dating? You have spent time with each other; you share the same or similar values, goals, and wants. You trust, respect, and care deeply for each other and, most importantly, you communicate well and feel safe with each other. This is when you can begin to discuss the terms of your dating relationship.

Answer the following questions about dating:

What will your parents think (no matter how old you are) about you dating? If you are under the age of 18, you may want to consult with your parents and/or guardians first to see if they feel you are old enough for dating.

My parents/guardian think:

_____

_____

Are you ready to hold hands, kiss, and take responsibility for how your actions and words can impact someone else?

Decide what you are ready for and list those items here:

_____

_____

How much time and what kind of commitment can you devote to the relationship? Think about this seriously.

_____

_____

If you want to meet someone what steps do you need to take in order for your parents/guardians to trust you with your boyfriend or girlfriend?

_____

_____

Are you looking for a companion—someone to go to events with and go out with once in a while?

_____

_____

> **Snail Trails…**
>
> Peter, 17 years old, had liked Angela since 1st grade. He finally got up the courage to ask her out. Angela, also 17, was surprised but was not interested in Peter as a boyfriend. She didn't want to hurt his feelings, so they went out. After two weeks of dating, Angela was just not interested in Peter as a boyfriend. She had shared that information with her friends and online. Peter's friends saw the online posts and told him. Peter was crushed.

How could have Angela shared her true feelings with Peter?

_____

_____

 Snail Talk

Angela should have been honest with Peter from the beginning and shared that she was more interested in just being friends and doing things together as friends.

Activity

Triangle

Jennifer, Josh, and Samantha are all friends. Both Jennifer and Samantha have a crush on Josh and want to ask him to the dance. Through open and honest communication, Jennifer and Samantha were able to work out staying friends.

What would you do if you find yourself liking the same person that your best friend likes?

_____

_____

Chapter 8

Deal Breakers

The Five Deal Breakers

Deal Breakers

There are dos and don'ts and deal breakers in all relationships between two or more people. Sometimes through our experiences, we learn that there are things that people do, that violate our values and what is most important to us. We refer to these as **Deal Breakers**. Eventually we all develop our own list of **Deal Breakers**. Hopefully, we learn to look for the things that caused our past relationships to end and try to avoid these things in future relationships.

When it comes to relationships in general and to dating relationships in particular, there are **Five** categories of behaviors that should always be **Deal Breakers**. You must avoid people who engage in any of these behaviors in order to protect yourself. These categories must make it to your own list of things to avoid because they are what destroy people and relationships universally.

People who display these behaviors typically need professional help and not a date. We must also mention that if you have ever personally known or are related to anyone who fits any one or more of the following categories, please seek professional help to make sure that you were not harmed in anyway.

The Five Deal Breakers

You should avoid anyone who behaves in ANY one or more of the following ways in their relationship with you or in their previous relationships (unless they have had professional help):

1. **Abusive Behaviors:** Any current or past actions that can harm you or others physically, verbally, psychologically, emotionally, socially, financially, virtually or sexually.

2. **Addictive Behaviors:** Any current or past abuse of or addiction to alcohol, prescription drugs, illicit drugs, gambling, sex, pornography (virtual, online or in person).

3. **Unethical:** Lack of integrity, lying, stealing, infidelity, cheating sexually or emotionally in the current relationship or a history of infidelity in previous relationships.

4. **Unlawful Behaviors:** Any current or past actions that are considered to be illegal or criminal.

5. **Unsafe Behaviors:** Any current or past actions that puts anyone in harm's way physically, psychologically, emotionally, verbally, socially, financially, virtually or sexually.

How do the five **Deal Breakers** help you find the right person?

☐ They list the five things that should be looked for and avoided in relationships.

☐ They are things to think about for my protection.

☐ They prevent unhealthy relationships.

Snail Wisdom

Remember, no amount of love will change a person and make the Deal Breakers go away. It will take professional help, and that will ONLY work if the person wants to change. It is important to set realistic expectations in any relationship so that you and your significant other understand what to expect and what is expected in daily interactions.

So what are realistic expectations?

Having and setting **realistic expectations** means that you understand that dogs don't meow and cats don't bark! In other words, people find it very difficult to change who they are. So we must be realistic and expect others to behave in a manner that is consistent with who they are.

Let's review...

It is very difficult for people to change their ways.

- If you meet someone who doesn't make you happy, they may never make you happy.
- If you meet someone who isn't polite and kind to you, they may never be polite and kind.
- If you meet someone who isn't generous, they may never be generous.

You must remember that **you** are responsible for your happiness and safety at all times! It is almost impossible for you to make anyone change.

After completing the features and personality charts in the chapter titled "Knowing What You Want" you have an idea of what is important to you. However, make sure that you take it slowly while you date. Those who move too quickly or focus on what they like often ignore **Pink Flags** that in time may become **Red Flags**.

Next, you will find a chart that will help you figure out **what to expect from someone based on the ways that they may be behaving**. These behaviors may also be considered **Red Flags** or warning signs and should cause you to investigate more or avoid the person all together. As the number of the following traits increases in someone's behavior, so does the likelihood that the relationship you have with them will be challenging.

If you observe your date behaving in one or more of the following ways towards others...	You may expect this from them in your relationship at some point ...
Arrogant, "better than others" attitude and behavior	Lack of consideration for you or others
Being mean is seen as cool	Lack of empathy for how you feel, and mean spirited
Secretive behaviors	Hiding things from you, not open
Acting jealous	Insecure, controlling, and distrustful
Being rude or mean to service people, kids, or animals	Anger management issues, lack of empathy disrespectful
Tight with money, time, & sharing	Emotionally unavailable, selfishness
Boasting about or being openly violent	Anger management problems, physically violent
Boasting about or being in a gang and wanting you to follow	Problems with law, drugs, violence, group thinking, and gang involvement
Boasting about getting high, drunk, or dealing drugs	Addiction and alcohol/drug abuse and dysfunctional home life
Using and abusing drugs, alcohol, prescription, and over-the-counter medications	Addiction and substance abuse, long term physical, psychological, and interpersonal problems

If you observe your date behaving in one or more of the following ways towards others…	You may expect this from them in your relationship at some point …
Acting entitled	Demanding, selfish, and unreasonable
Bullying	Violence and disrespect towards you
Boasting about scamming, cheating, lying and getting away with things	Lack of personal integrity, and social personality, and emotional dysfunction
Poor relationship with parents/siblings	Poor/unstable relationship with you and others
Dysfunctional family life	Dysfunctional personal life
Reactive and impulsive behaviors, reckless driving	Dangerous, reckless decisions that can harm you or others
Promiscuous and hypersexual	Unable to delay gratification, poor decision making, STDs
Poor school performance	Indicates problem in some area

> **Snail Trail...**
>
> Derik, 16 years old, and Sandy, 15 years old, met online through Social Media. They had been using instant messaging to keep their new relationship private. They spoke online sometimes as many as four or five times a day. They really seemed to be getting along well. It was a dream come true for Sandy because she had always been shy. After about a week, Sandy shared her phone number with Derik and their relationship began to grow as they spoke more often through text, online, and phone calls.
>
> After about three weeks, both Derik and Sandy decided to meet at a local movie theatre for a 7:00 p.m. movie. They also decided to meet in the parking lot of the movie theatre after they were dropped off so they could decide if they really wanted to see a movie or not. Sandy had told her parents that she was meeting girl friends and that her movie would get out at 10:00 p.m.

Please identify any **Pink Flags** and any of the **Five Principles of Healthy Decision Making** that Sandy and Derik ignored:

_____

_____

 Snail Talk

Both Sandy and Derik should have checked one another out through their mutual friends. They shouldn't have kept their relationship a secret but instead should have opened their relationship to their friends to determine if both were telling the truth about their age and who they were.

Sandy should not have lied to her parents because if anything goes wrong, her parents would have false information. Her lying should also be a **Pink Flag** to Derik as it may indicate Sandy's comfort with lying to her parents or in general.

Never meet someone in a private or secluded setting whom you've not met before, because that puts you in a vulnerable position. Always tell someone you know and trust, who you plan on meeting and where the meeting will be. In fact, if it is a new person that you've never met and your friends have never met, for your safety you should always meet in a public place. Always bring a friend or friends along and have an exit plan of some sort. Your exit plan could be to have a friend join you after 15 minutes or have a friend call you to ensure your safety. Make sure you have your own ride home.

> **Snail Trail...**
>
> Carol met Blake through a dating service. They agreed to meet at a restaurant for their first date. During the date, Blake began bragging about how he beats other people up for fun. He then grabbed Carol's arm roughly and shared that he enjoys watching people flinch.

Please identify any **Pink Flags** and any of the **Five Deal Breakers** that Carol must recognize:

_____

_____

Say this to yourself three times: **RELATIONSHIPS ARE BUILT SLOWLY AND OVER TIME.**

Think about exit plans… What could your exit plan be if you were on a first date? You meet in a public place and your parents know where you are. You have a bad feeling about the person you are with. He/she was bragging about beating people up. How would you get out of the date? What is your exit plan?

_____

_____

Let's review…

No matter where you go or where you're meeting someone new or someone you don't know very well, you should always have a plan to get out of the meeting in case you are uncomfortable or are sensing **Pink Flags**.

Have your parent, guardian, or friend call you every hour or so while you are on the date. Develop a secret code word or sentence with your parent, guardian, or friend that tells them that you would like to end the meeting: for example you can ask, "How's grandma?" Then you can end your meeting by telling your date that your grandma is sick and you must go home.

Snail Trail…

Karen really wants to have as much sex with as many boys as possible, and Christian wants to find and marry his sweetheart. Christian sees Karen's sexual attraction towards him as a sign of love.

Christian believes that if he can make Karen fall in love with him, she will eventually want what he wants; she will want to get married and begin a life together. However, Karen is planning on not getting married and staying single for a very long time. For her, Christian is the hottest boy, and her friends have dared her to ask him out and get lucky.

What are the **Pink Flags?**

_____

_____

Snail Talk

It is very difficult or impossible to make someone fall in love with you. Once Christian realizes that Karen wants a different type of relationship than he does at this time, he needs to walk away.

Christian would like a long-term committed relationship, and Karen doesn't. She would like to have many relationships. Learning what each person in the relationship wants is part of the investigative process. Christian and Karen have both come to a point in their relationship where they both want different things. They need to accept this and instead agree to be friends rather than dating partners.

Let's review…

Approach dating seriously and make sure that you are prepared to handle all the aspects of the relationship. You must think logically and always ask yourself, "Is what I am doing safe and in my best interest?"

Setting realistic expectations in a **Healthy Relationship** requires knowing yourself and the desire to discover and learn about the other. Setting realistic expectations is like buying something. **It is the ability to figure out what the relationship with the person you are considering will cost you and then deciding on whether or not you can afford it.**

Snail Talk

People who describe their relationships, both friendships and dating, as positive, feel connected, both physically and emotionally. They typically have a great deal in common such as similar values, backgrounds, interests, direction, and goals. The more a couple has in common with each other and the more they accept each other's differences while supporting personal goals, the more satisfying their relationship will be.

Once you have committed to a relationship, communicate openly, honestly, directly, and promptly. Don't let concerns grow into problems. Too often people avoid honest communication because they are afraid to say something wrong, hurt someone, or start a fight. Don't over think the relationship; instead, set mutual boundaries and intentions at the beginning of the relationship and check in with each other on a regular basis to make sure that things are going well and that there are no unspoken problems.

These agreements and check points will help to build trust. You must realize that violating and abusing these agreements are a clear break in trust and will damage your relationship. Remember, dating is an investigative process and your safety needs to be top priority in order for the relationship to work.

 Snail Wisdom

Dig deep when investigating relationships, but stay out of the hole.

To be investigative in a relationship, you are looking at the person through a magnifying glass to see if they have the same values, belief system, boundaries, and intentions. This process takes time - it can take over a year. As we mentioned before, you need to talk about the rules by which you will interact with each other and decide on your relationship's **Code of Conduct**.

James and Kelly were friends and shared many of the same values. As part of James' investigation, he had decided that he would spend a lot of time getting to know Kelly by hanging out with her family and friends. He really liked Kelly's friends and family and, in a short time, was treated like part of the family. He was invited to dinner and events.

After a year, James and Kelly had so much in common that they were being thought of as inseparable and belonging together. Their commitment to the relationship grew stronger and together they worked on developing the same values and shared goals.

 Snail Talk

Creating memories with one another's friends and family helps to create common interest. These common interests help the couple feel closer and more connected.

Here is James and Kelly's **Code of Conduct.** They created this together in stages as they were going through the different phases of their **Healthy Relationship**.

1. Mutual consent on decisions that impact our relationship and us.

2. Truth at all costs. No lying.

3. No alcohol or drug use.

4. Sex, when the reason, time and place is mutually discussed, agreed upon, right and safe for both parties.

5. Respect one another's decisions and never make one another feel guilty for not agreeing. Instead agree to disagree.

6. Agree on priorities; school, family, significant other, friends.

7. Respect privacy by not sharing our secrets and experiences with others even after a break up.

What do you want your **Code of Conduct** to be?

_____

_____

_____

_____

_____

_____

_____

_____

_____

How many chances should you give the relationship if the code is broken?

_____

_____

_____

Chapter 9

It's More Than T.R.U.S.T.

Gathering Information for your Safety

It's More than T.R.U.S.T.

Life is full of risks and, while dating, it is extremely important to realize that your safety must come first. **RELATIONSHIPS ARE BUILT SLOWLY AND OVER TIME.** So, plan on being safe by following these simple rules and use the acronym **T.R.U.S.T.** to keep these rules in mind.

T= Trust your gut and talk to someone. Listen to your inner voice. If you don't feel right or safe, STOP and check out your thoughts with an adult you trust.

Think about situations or times where you didn't listen to your inner voice. What happened?

_____

_____

_____

R= Respect yourself and the person that you are meeting. Only do things on the first date that you won't regret later.

List some of the things that you might do on a first date that you may regret later:

_____

_____

_____

U= Understand who you are meeting before you meet: ask your friends about the person. Ask his or her friends about the person. Do a background check of some sort.

List some of the resources you can use to check someone's background:

_____

_____

_____

S= Safety comes first. On the first few dates a double date would be safer. Always meet in public places. Do not get into his or her car on the first few dates, and make certain that the person that you are meeting is who he/she says he/she is.

List some ways you can create a "safe" dating experience:

_____

_____

_____

T=Tell someone the 5 "Ws" of your plans: Who, what, when, where, why and when again:

_____

_____

_____

For example: I am going with John to the movies tonight from 7:00 p.m. to 9:00 p.m. for a date and I should be home by 9:30 p.m. Make arrangements to call/text your parent/guardian when you get to your destination and again when you are about to go to another place or go home. Make certain that your cell phone is well charged and always have an exit plan, especially on the first date. Remember, always have your own ride home.

Another example: If you are on a first or second date, ask a friend or parent to call/text you after the first half hour and then again throughout the date. As shared in the chapter "Safety First", always prepare an exit plan with parent/guardian prior to leaving your home. Agree on a secret word or phrase that you can use if the date is not going well.

For your own safety, if it is an option, take a friend/family member with you on the first couple of dates.

Snail Wisdom

Another important thing you must keep in mind is that investigators ask many questions and really listen well. It is important that you listen well and look for Pink Flags.

Gathering Information for your Safety

Here are some questions to ask someone as you are getting to know them. You don't have to ask all of these questions at the same time. They will help you gather information that may help you in determining your safety in the relationship:

- Have you ever dated before? If so, when, why, and how did it end?

- Are you still friends with the person you broke up with?

- How did you handle conflict in your relationships?

- How does your family deal with conflict and anger?

- What do you do when you get angry?

- What do you do to have fun?

- Do you drink/smoke/like to get high?

- What are your **Deal Breakers**? What would make you end a relationship?

- Have you ever ended a relationship or been dumped in the past? If so, why?

- What is the best way to break up with someone?

These and other questions can help you get an idea as to how relationships and conflicts are handled in the family of the person that you are with. They may help you learn about the other person's coping tools and relationship patterns.

Write down other questions that you may want to ask:

_____

_____

_____

_____

Red Flags:

Any answer to the above questions or the questions that you have created, that show any signs at all of the **Five Deal Breakers** (such as abuse, lying, cheating, etc., that we have discussed already), should be seen as **Red Flags.** You are actually collecting stories about each other and looking for patterns in these stories. The more that the stories are about problems, conflict, pain, and broken relationships, that haven't been worked out, the stronger the likelihood of similar things developing in your relationship with each other.

What should you do if your story has these themes? Seek professional help: speak to your school psychologist or counselor and ask your parents to obtain similar support for you. You can learn to stop old behaviors, break old patterns, and learn better ways to cope.

List some questions from our list that you plan on asking:

_____

_____

_____

Snail Wisdom

Bad things happen to good people. Safety is always your first priority. Always apply the Five Principles of Healthy Decision Making!

Here are some additional tips that may save you and your life:

1. If you can, find out something about the person that you are interested in dating. Ask your friends what they know about the person. Try to find someone in common who can tell you about the person's character and values. Speak with an adult that you trust. Conduct a cyber check by friending him/her on social media.

2. Be mindful of what you share electronically. Remember that e-mail, text and posts **live forever** and can create messy problems in future relationships.

3. Always **tell** someone where you are going and who will be with you.

4. Until you trust this person, for the first few months, always date in **public places.**

5. Plan activities with **friends and family** at first.

6. Attend prearranged events: school/community dances, religious events, restaurants, coffee shops, ice cream shops, study groups, and movies.

7. Always have your phone fully charged prior to going on the date.

8. Buy your own drink and don't leave it unattended. Don't share drinks.

9. Don't accept drinks from opened containers or leave your drink unattended. It is extremely easy to add drugs and substances to your drink that will make you helpless, powerless and vulnerable.

10. Always have an EXIT plan and do not give your car keys or personal belongings to anyone. Have an agreement with your parent or someone who cares about you to "Pick you up, no matter what time of day or night with no questions asked."

11. Avoid attending parties/gatherings where you don't know anyone.

12. **Do not** let anyone who is drunk or under the influence drive you.

13. **Do not** let anyone who is carrying/selling/dealing drugs drive you.

14. Never leave a public place with the new person that you've just met, even if it's to go and get something from the car that belongs to either one of you.

15. Never get into a car where there are a bunch of people you don't know.

Let's review…

For your safety always listen to your GUT and never be persuaded by peer pressure or temptations. Make sure that you think through and ask yourself what is the best and the worst thing that can happen on this date. Always play through these scenarios that are both good and bad in your head, so that you are not surprised. Always think about an exit plan before you enter a situation.

Say this to yourself three times: **RELATIONSHIPS ARE BUILT SLOWLY AND OVER TIME.**

Activity

Dating what ifs?

Imagine the scenario below where good things can go wrong. Now write about what can go wrong for each listed item and why.

First date: on a sail boat:

_____

_____

_____

First date: at the movies in which the movie has not been jointly selected:

___

First date: at your date's parents' home when no one is there:

___

Your date makes you do something that you are uncomfortable with:

___

Your date grabs your arm real hard:

___

Your date drinks alcohol to get drunk:

___

There are several places to avoid while getting to know the other person and developing trust in your new relationship.

- Parks and secluded places, especially at night.

- Cars, vans, RVs, boats, and all modes of transportation, especially when you don't have CONTROL and are not the operator.

- Private places where there are no other people, such as his/her bedroom, apartment, dorm room, or friend's house.

There are personality styles that usually cause heartache and pain; consequently, you need to be aware of them in order to protect yourself and your heart. As you go about your investigation, if you find out that the person that you're interested in has one or more of the following characteristics, reconsider your decision to move forward and be careful:

- People who are involved with the use/sale/exchange of drugs at any level.

- People who are abusing alcohol/illegal/prescription drugs.

- People who have a fascination with weapons and hurting others.

- People who have criminal histories and problems with the law.

- People who are depressed or preoccupied with suicidal thoughts. Please remember these people need professional attention. It is very important that you inform a responsible adult promptly.

- People who are members of gangs, cults, or groups that hate and exclude those who belong to other groups.

- People who have chaotic lives and relationships and who engage in destructive behaviors as a way of dealing with their circumstances (e.g. cutting themselves).

- People who "blow up" easily and have a history of violence (beating others up or getting into fights).

- People who are possessive and may want you to abandon your family, friends, and anything that is important to you or brings you joy.

- People who are cruel or mean to animals and children and have no regard or respect for others or their property.

- People who have a fascination with setting fires.

- People who have severe psychological problems and are not getting professional help.

The above people should be seeking and receiving professional help before they are suitable for a **Healthy Relationship.**

Chapter 10

Physical Intimacy

Finding and Being the Right Person

Physical Intimacy

You must build a **Healthy Relationship** before physical intimacy. Sex should be the absolute final way that you communicate your care and love for another. It is truly the icing on the cake. You can't put the icing on if you are just acquaintances. Despite what you see on television and in the media, you must remember it is more harmful than helpful to jump into sex without appropriate and adequate investigation.

If you want to have a deeper relationship than just being sexually attracted to one another, you need to spend time learning about each other as you **communicate openly, build trust, build respect and create mutual intentions.** You must discuss your personal **Code of Conduct** and agree on the terms of your relationship.

Sex needs to be saved for the **right person**, the **right time,** and the **right place**. Do not rush into sex; think about it and develop a common plan with your partner. Do not give in to pressure, even if it means breaking up. Remember, you will have this memory for the rest of your life, so pick the **right person, the right place,** and **the right time.**

What does the right person mean to you?

Finding and Being the Right Person

Remember what the **SNAIL** stood for? The right person is someone who:

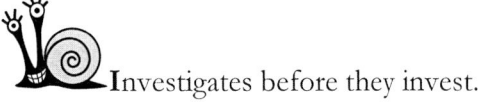Slows down and seeks to understand you and themselves. They set expectations.

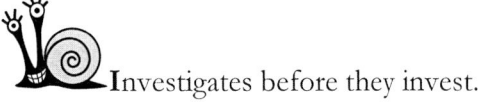Negotiates the terms and goals of your relationship.

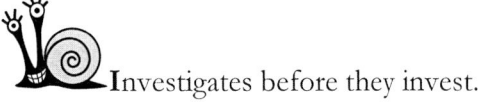Asks about how their choices and behavior will impact the relationship. Attend to **Pink Flags** and **Red Flags**.

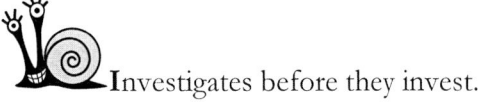Investigates before they invest.

 Listens to their gut, the other person's words, and actions.

The right person is someone who thinks of your best interest as if it is his/hers. At times the right person may even put your needs ahead of his/hers. This person will suggest things like "I want this to be the most special event for both of us." Or "I only want to if you do, and we can take as long as we want to make that decision." Or "We should both feel really good about this decision."

The right person will not try and coax you into having sex and will not attempt to engage you physically against your will. The right person is the one who says: "I think if we have sex now it would really complicate things and we are too young and our parents won't approve."

List what would make a person be the right person for you:

_____

_____

Your first sexual experience, the circumstances, and the relationship that leads to sex will affect all the relationships in your life. If the first experience makes you feel valued, cherished, special, and loved, then you will continue to have positive experiences.

 Snail Talk

If you feel manipulated, taken advantage of, used, cheapened, unloved, and not valued, it may take a lifetime to correct these experiences. Some folks never recover and continue to repeat the same pattern over and over again. This is one of the reasons why dating is an investigative process, because you are looking for someone with whom to share your most valuable possession, and that is **YOU**. So investigate and look for **the right person**.

List what makes you special:

_____

_____

List how you honor, respect, and cherish yourself:

_____

_____

List how your parents or adults in your life honor, respect, and cherish you:

___

___

Snail Wisdom

You must honor, respect, and cherish yourself before expecting it from others.

If you investigate before you invest, in the event of a break-up, the **Shared Respect** and **Trust** that you have jointly created will let you end things with as little trauma and drama as possible. You will be able to end the relationship, feeling sad for it being over, but feeling glad for having known each other.

If you both look at dating as an investigative process, you are able to identify and work towards what you both want.

What does "the right time" mean to you?

___

___

> **Let's review...**
>
> Things are better when done in **SNAIL** time and **SNAIL** manner. Build your relationship on a strong friendship and understand each other's personality and goals. Take time to build your relationship before having sex! Time together is needed to build trust and discuss and exchange ideas to set the terms of the relationship and create the **Code of Conduct**. Time is needed to learn about each other and decide on what the mutual goals are for the couple and the relationship.

Snail Wisdom

Sex is an adult act with adult consequences and the couple must be aware of and willing to deal with these consequences. Having sex does not make you an adult.

The three most common results of rushing into unplanned and poorly-timed sex are: **sexually transmitted diseases (STDs), pregnancy** and **broken hearts. STDs** can be incurable and some can kill you. **Unwanted pregnancy** has emotional, ethical, social, legal, financial, and life-altering consequences. Some **broken hearts** never mend. This is why the **right time** is when the couple is able to understand, cope, and deal with the many consequences of sex, independently of their parents!

Let's review…

Right time is when one person says to the other: "Neither one of us could handle a **pregnancy** in any way right now, so let's wait awhile and do other things."

Right time means understanding and accepting that no contraceptive method is 100% effective and that if you engage in adult behaviors, you must be ready for adult consequences.

What does the right place mean to you?

_____

_____

Remember, you will have this memory for a lifetime. When someone asks you in your forties: what was the first time you had sex and where did it take place? What would you rather say: "Oh, it was with this person I hardly knew; we were both drunk after a football game and it was behind the couch in his/her family room, or the back seat of his/her father's car"? Or, would you rather say, "It was an amazing time, we were so in love and we planned it out for such a long time and it was at this amazing place…I will never forget it"?

Learn as much as you can about the person, and ALWAYS apply the **Five Principles of Healthy Decision Making** to the choices that you are considering in your dating relationship.

Snail Wisdom

Be prepared, learn as much as you can about your body and realize that sharing your body through sex is a privilege that must be earned.

Let's review…

Some **SNAIL**s throw love darts at each other when aroused. They are responsible for what they throw and HOW they CHOOSE to respond to the darts thrown at them.

You are not responsible for your partner's arousal. You are each responsible for your own arousal and for taking care of it in a way that is considered respectful and appropriate by both of you.

It's okay to say "No." Guys can say, "No," too. Hearing "No" does not make you unlovable or undesirable. It simply means the right conditions are absent. When you both feel you are with the right person, at the right time, and in the right place, then each of you will *willingly* say "Yes."

Until then, you have to continue the investigative process. Once you are ready to make a real commitment to each other, and have discussed and exchanged your **Code of Conduct,** there are many ways to move forward with the physical investigative process.

Snail Wisdom

Popularity, desirability, and self worth are not determined by your ability to "turn another person on."

Snail Trail…

Yolanda and Sean have been dating for about six months. They are boyfriend and girlfriend, and Yolanda is telling everyone that they are lovers.

Snail Talk

Yolanda needs to be more careful when picking her words. The term lovers usually refers to people who have a sexual relationship with each other. Yolanda and Sean are just beginning to develop and investigate their relationship, and they are not yet sexual. Remember **RELATIONSHIPS ARE BUILT SLOWLY AND OVER TIME.** To become sexual with someone is a very important decision that requires investigation, communication, and commitment.

Yolanda is better off referring to Sean as her good friend or her boyfriend.

What will you do if your partner wants to become sexual before you are ready?

_____

_____

Do you remember the "Five Principles of Healthy Decision Making?"

1. **It must be Legal:** Is the decision and its consequences (outcome) legal? Would you get into trouble with the law?

2. **It must be Ethical:** Is the decision and its consequences morally right or wrong? If your choice was disclosed to others would it embarrass you or your family?

3. **It must be Safe at all levels:** Is the decision and its consequences safe?

    a- Physiologically safe (body): How will it affect my/our/another's physical health and well being?

    b- Psychologically safe (mind): How will it affect my/our/another's psychological/emotional well being?

    c- Socially safe: How will it affect my/ours/others social situations and social well being?

    d- Spiritually safe. How will it affect my/our/another's spiritual life?

4. **It must be Appropriate:** Given my role(s) and responsibilities, if someone took a photo of me/us doing what I/we have decided to do: "Will I/we be okay and proud to have it appear on the nightly news?" or "Will I/we be embarrassed and want to leave town?"

5. **It must be aligned with your Value system**(s): Is the decision and its consequences in alignment with my/your/our personal and familial values? Would you tell your parents?

Here are the "Five Principles of Healthy Decision Making" as applied to becoming sexual with someone.

Is it **legal** to have sex with this person, and what will be the legal consequences?

List some of the legal consequences of having sex with the wrong person, at a wrong place, and at a wrong time:

_____

_____

Is it morally **right or wrong?** (Here are some questions that can help you examine this principle: Is the person single? Are you seeing someone else? Is the decision to have sex and its consequences morally right or wrong?)

_____

_____

List some of the consequences of having sex with the wrong person, at a wrong place, and at a wrong time:

_____

_____

Is it **safe?** (physical and emotional consequences, contraception used, socially safe, financially safe, no STDs, etc.)

List some of the physical and emotional consequences of having sex with the wrong person, at a wrong place, and at a wrong time:

_____

_____

Is it **appropriate?** Ask yourself: Is what I am doing appropriate? Would I be embarrassed or in trouble if someone took a photo of me and this person? Or, "Will I or we be embarrassed and want to leave town?"

List some of the social consequences of having sex with the wrong person, at a wrong place, and at a wrong time that may become public knowledge:

_____

_____

Is it aligned with my **Value** system: Is the decision to have sex now and its consequences, with this person and in these circumstances, in alignment with my personal, family, and social values?

List some negatives about having sex when it is not aligned to your value system:

_____

_____

Chapter 11

Parent/Guardian Advice

Parent /Guardian Advice

Parents need to create and maintain **Healthy Relationships** with each other and their children. This means that they communicate their needs, concerns, and disagreements openly, respectfully, and directly. Parents and families need to think and operate as a team. We mentioned earlier that how a couple works together to achieve their shared goals and intentions is like two gardeners that work together to create the garden that they both desire to have. When parents disrespect each other, harbor resentments, or do not make amends and are ineffective at resolving conflict, children internalize interpersonal patterns and will carry them out in their lives. When parents are positive role models for their son/daughter as they engage in healthy interactions and look for ways to encourage healthy decision making, they are in essence ensuring that their son or daughter is safe and successful in their relationships.

Getting to know your son's or daughter's friend is the best way to create a safe environment to see how you can best support your child as he/she interacts with their peers. Inviting and including your child's friend(s)/date (and sometimes even their family) into your home can help you identify potential areas of concern that you can focus on as you coach your son or daughter. Inviting your child's friend(s)/date over to your home for the first several get-togethers can also enable you to supervise without hovering.

> **Snail Trail...**
>
> Janet and Bob were on their second date at Janet's home. They were sitting on the couch when Janet leaned closely to Bob and kissed him while you, the parents, are in clear view.

How do you feel about this? What is your reaction?

_____

_____

_____

How should you respond?

_____

_____

_____

Snail Talk

You may have mixed feelings and this may be a good opportunity to ask Janet and Bob if they are aware of the impact that their behavior may have on other people. You may also ask them to guess how you are feeling about it. On the other hand, you may do better to step away and have a discussion with your son or daughter later.

What you don't want to do is to embarrass or humiliate the couple. What they are doing is part of human nature, although it may be against some value systems. Ask yourself this: is the couple engaged in an action that is aligned with our family values and, if so, is the timing and location appropriate?

Safety is a family matter.

Snail Wisdom

If you engage in unsafe behaviors, so will your children.

Always make sure that you know where your son or daughter is. Make sure that your son or daughter leaves the home with a fully charged cell phone and knows how to use it. Set up rules that include having your son or daughter call you every hour or so to provide you with an update. Be sure to develop a safety plan in advance of your child leaving the house so that if the date becomes uncomfortable he/she knows what to do.

Practice the safety plan many times. It is very important that your child knows that if they ever find themselves in a troubling situation, they can call you without the fear of consequences. So many tragedies can be prevented if children and young adults felt comfortable calling an adult who they believed would help them and not be mad for the situation that they had created.

Young adults typically have strong emotions that may change rapidly, especially while dating, because the experiences are so new and can be so very intense. Your son or daughter may have never have had strong feelings for another person and break ups can be devastating and life altering. For these reasons it is essential that your son or daughter have an open relationship and an on-going dialogue with a parent or a trusted adult with whom they can share concerns and ask questions. Parents can be effective teachers if they can share their stories sincerely.

Start by sharing your first dating experiences.

1. What was the name of the person with whom you shared your first date?

2. Where did you meet?

3. Where did you go?

4. How long did the relationship last? How and why did it end?

5. What did you learn from the relationship?

6. What would you do differently if you could go back?

> **Snail Trail...**
>
> Samantha and Nick are both in their 20s and have been dating in school for awhile. They are trying to set up a meet and greet so that Samantha's parents will trust them. Samantha's parents will not allow dating.

 **Snail Talk**

If the young adults are making healthy decisions and doing the right thing, then they should be given a chance. As parents, you can set boundaries and provide information regarding relationships and sex. Engage your child in discussing these topics so that you can agree to a family **Code of Conduct**. The more open and transparent parents are with their children, and the more honesty they encourage within their family, the more successful and effective the child will be in his/her relationship with others. Remember, when children sneak around, everyone loses. Don't make your home a place that your child wants to run away from.

Chapter 12

Wrapping it Up

Wrapping it Up

Dating is a serious journey that can have lifelong consequences. How you handle yourself in the early and exploratory phases will stay with you for a lifetime. If you are a teenager or an adult and you want to begin to investigate relationships then do just that: investigate. Use the stages listed in the chapter *Relationships Take Time* and be serious with your process. Work and build your relationship together through the stages and realize that the result will be the development of a strong and meaningful relationship.

The stages in *Relationships Take Time* were presented to make you aware that long-lasting friendships and love does not happen overnight. In fact, relationships may take a lifetime of continuous exploration and fine tuning with every interaction and experience the couple shares.

We've used the example of concentric rings and snails to develop the idea that relationships happen over time and there is a process to ensure success. Each stage is fluid and interrelated with multiple layers that include experiences and reactions. How well a couple relates, interacts, and faces challenges with each other is what determines successful, durable, and long-lived relationships.

There are four simple rules that ensure the success of any relationship.

1. Be trustworthy: stand by what you say.
2. Be respectful: consider the impact that your words, actions, and decisions have on others.
3. Communicate openly and honestly: make sure that what you think, say, and do are all aligned.
4. Work towards shared goals: work together to get there.

These four simple rules set the stage for any healthy and long lasting relationship.

One of the main themes of this workbook is your safety. Safety needs to be your priority. You need to feel comfortable and confident while you explore **Healthy Relationships**. If at any time you're not comfortable in your relationship, then you need to consult with a trusted adult or advisor and possibly even end the relationship.

In *Relationships Take Time*, there is also list of healthy decision-making principles. These principles are meant to be used not only with dating relationships but also with any decision that you are considering. Applying them can save you a great deal of pain, drama, and heartache.

Pink Flags and **Red Flags** were mentioned to help you understand that you need to recognize the things that don't feel right to you. When **Pink Flags** or **Red Flags** are experienced, you need to address them through open and honest communication. If you are experiencing **Pink** and or **Red Flags** in a relationship, most likely it isn't okay—you deserve better! **Deal Breakers** need to be adhered to in order to avoid heartache. Revisit chapter 8 to refresh your memory on the **Five Deal Breakers.**

Developing a **Code of Conduct** is an important component of a **Healthy Relationship**. Don't be afraid to negotiate your code up front. Determine what it is that you are comfortable doing and discuss this with your dating partner. It is okay just to want to hold hands. No one should ever be pressured into doing anything that they are unwilling to do. So, make your preferences clear from the beginning and at anytime when you feel uncomfortable.

Finally, remember our mascot the **SNAIL**. A **SNAIL** moves its way through life very slowly. The **SNAIL** does leave a path and that is its history. The path that it leaves behind shows where it has been. You too will carry your dating history to every relationship that you experience. Remember being the right person is just as important as finding the right person. Now go be your best and find what you deserve. Remember, always have fun and laugh a lot.

At our workshops, we have asked our participants to describe what dating is for them in a sentence.

He doesn't show his heart because he has insurance.

Just when I think I'm in love, I break up.

Be trustful, honest, caring, and funny.

I take chances to look for the one.

I'm socially awkward and don't have a boyfriend.

I'm still waiting for my prince.

It is like living in a castle.

My boyfriend and I have been together for over a year.

Love lasts with honesty.

I enjoy going out to restaurants with my dates.

And finally some tidbits about us…

Tarane Sondoozi is a well sought after speaker, master story teller, organizational consultant and author. She holds a doctorate degree in clinical psychology from United States International University in San Diego, CA. She has over 29 years of extensive experience in clinical and organizational settings, developing and providing trainings that foster personal and professional growth and success. She is the mother of 3 amazing daughters.

Diana Loiewski is a professional speaker, teacher, and writer. She is also a mother of 3 amazing daughters who inspire her every day. She attended Southern Connecticut State University and earned a BS in Special Education and a Masters in English. She also holds an Administrative Credential and Crosscultural, Language, and Academic Development (CLAD) Certificate. Teaching is her first passion and she has been working in the field of Special Education since 1975. She brings a joy and enthusiasm to everything that she does.

Renee Tompkins is a Speech Language Pathologist. She received her BS and MS in Speech Language Pathology from Illinois State Und mother of two very active young boys. She currently works with 18-22 year o with an array of disabilities and amazing abilities! Many of her students were a huge inspiration for this book.

Miriam Larson was raised in Philadelphia, Pennsylvania. At an early age art became her passion. She started a lifelong career in art by receiving a BS in Art Education from The Pennsylvania State University. After meeting and marrying her husband, she settled with him in San Diego, California, to raise their son and daughter. She now teaches high school art and continues to work as a graphic artist. Coming from a family with disabilities, she is especially interested in her work with students with disabilities.

Conclusion & Acknowledgement

The Healthy Relationship workbook was created as a tool for young adults, parents and professionals who attend our workshops and trainings. We wish to thank our lucky stars for bringing us and our paths together. As parents, and teachers, we realized that sometimes we just need a little more support. We would like to thank our daughters Lauren, Jacqueline, Catherine, Natasha, Liliana, Fiona, Josie, and our sons Nick, Anthony, Michael, and their friends for answering our endless questions and for putting up with our writing and laughing fits.

We also would like to thank **Linda Loiewski** for her continual support, creative help, cover design, and amazing logo design. Linda is an art director who develops insightful and creative design solutions that reflect current trends. She is innovative, develops work for all business fields, and is able to meet the different needs and desires of all of her clients. Linda is the founder of LX2, a graphic art company in Hamden, Connecticut.

We look forward to your feedback, or questions. Please visit us at **talkcounts.com** and let us know what you think.